It's a Bunny-Eat-Bunny World

Walker & Company

New York

It's a Bunny-Eat-Bunny World

◆

A Writer's Guide to Surviving
and Thriving in Today's Competitive
Children's Book Market

◆

Olga Litowinsky

For Edward,

sempre a minha beira

First published in the United States of America
in 2001 by Walker Publishing Company, Inc.

Published simultaneously in Canada by
Fitzhenry and Whiteside, Markham, Ontario L3R 4T8

Library of Congress Cataloging-in-Publication Data

Litowinsky, Olga.
    It's a bunny-eat-bunny world : a writer's guide to
surviving and thriving in today's competitive
children's book market / Olga Litowinsky.
        p.   cm.
    Includes bibliographical references.
    ISBN 0-8027-8637-5 —
    ISBN 0-8027-7523-3 (pbk.)
    1. Children's literature—Authorship.   I. Title.

PN147.5 .L57   2001
808.06'8—dc21
                                        00-047317

Illustrations by Lonnie Sue Johnson

Book design by Jennifer Ann Daddio

Printed in the United States of America
2   4   6   8   10   9   7   5   3   1

Contents

Part I: Background

Part II: Foreground

Welcome to the
Rabbit Hole

✦

The word "impossible" is not in my dictionary
—Napoleon Bonaparte

A writer—let's call him Gus Casey—came up to me recently and said, "I've heard it's impossible for new writers to get a children's book published. Is that true?"

"It's more difficult than it used to be," I answered, "but it's not impossible."

Writers like Gus are worried and confused as we ease into the third millennium. Some even wonder whether the book itself will survive in the face of competition from electronic technology. History demonstrates it will, because in spite of the temptations of movies, television, video games, and computers, a place remains for Bound Orderly Organized Knowledge, otherwise known as the BOOK. In fact, more books for children are being published—and sold—than ever before. The demand for new books is high, and it is the writer who is the indispensable provider of information, enlightenment, and entertainment, or, as the media moguls say nowadays, "content."

However, to succeed in the dizzying Rabbit Hole world of children's book publishing, Gus will have to adjust to new ways. Much of what I wrote in my previous book, *Writing and Publishing Books for Children in the 1990s: The View from the Editor's Desk* (1992), remains relevant. For those who haven't read the first book, I repeat in this one the basic information about such matters as how to find a publisher and submit a manuscript.

Nonetheless, a great deal has changed since 1992, in the industry and in my own life. I was then an executive editor at Simon & Schuster. A few years later, with the advent of a new children's publisher, hired to engineer a major overhaul of the division, my job was eliminated. I decided to become a literary agent, which provided me with valuable insights into that field. And all along, I have been writing and trying to sell my own manuscripts, so I understand how writers feel about editors and publishers and reviewers, especially in these changing times.

To help writers understand how the children's market for books has changed, Part I: Background—the first four chapters—provides a brief history of children's publishing. In the beginning it was the invaluable and pioneering support of librarians and the growth of libraries that created the children's book industry. Everything we do today began with the librarians, and the library market remains the guiding inspiration for good children's books.

Important innovations during the past twenty-five years lead us to the present, where new ways coexist with the old. Recent developments include the rise of paperbacks and the mass market, which brought affordable books to more children; (2) the transformation of most of the former independent publishing firms into global media corporations; and (3) the rapid, widespread growth of chain and on-line bookstores.

Some readers may prefer to begin with Part II, Foreground. Chapters 5 through 9 provide material on how to write for children—taking into account genres and age levels. Chapters 10 to 15 are concerned with the business of publishing and deal with how to find a publisher, negotiate a contract, and market your work after publication.

Books are acquired and edited much as they always were. Writing for children remains a calling, a passion, a delight. And some writers have found that writing a successful children's book is as good as winning the lottery: sales and income have never been higher. As with Gus later in the book, it's my hope that you, the aspiring writer, will find your path to getting published successfully in this fast-changing world. The writer today must wear many hats, so hold on to all of them and jump right in!

ACKNOWLEDGMENTS

This book is based on my life after the age of six, when I learned to read. I've had a book nearby ever since. Most of my working life was spent in publishing, and I wish to express my appreciation to my first mentors, under whom I served my apprenticeship, Erik Wensberg of the Columbia University *Forum* and Carolyn Trager of Crowell-Collier Press. After that came the writers and colleagues I've worked with—a long list from A to Z—who also inspired and informed me.

Most recently, my former editor, Bebe Willoughby, sustained me through the writing of *It's a Bunny-Eat-Bunny World* with her comments and good sense, and I'm grateful to her, Edward Babun, Don Hinkle, and Carol Carrick for reading the early drafts of the manuscript and pointing out places for improvement. I also wish to thank all the people who spoke to me about the state of writing and publishing today and who are quoted in the book.

Finally, I am grateful to Marilyn Marlow, my agent, and to Soyung Pak and Emily Easton, my editors, for their patience and guidance while I was writing *It's a Bunny-Eat-Bunny World*. They are proof that publishing remains a noble endeavor.

PART I

✦

Background

1

The Bunny Also Rises

✦

THE BEGINNINGS OF CHILDREN'S
PUBLISHING IN AMERICA

When one door is shut, another opens.
—Miguel de Cervantes

Born during the Great Depression, I grew up in an immigrant family in Newark, New Jersey, and longed to be part of the small-town world shown in movies like *The Music Man* or performed in now-forgotten radio shows like *Henry Aldrich.* My mother loved the way Mrs. Aldrich called, at the beginning of each show, "Hen-RY! Henry AL-drich!" It wasn't too different from the way she called her children to come home from the streets where we roller-skated, played hide-and-seek, stickball, and marbles. Later, most of my generation moved to the suburbs in pursuit of the American dream as exemplified by a white frame house with a picket fence on Elm Street. No matter where they live, parents still call to their children the way Mrs. Aldrich and my mother called to theirs. Nonetheless, an era has ended.

Historians agree that people living in the twentieth century witnessed more changes than people in any other period of human history. When my father, who was born in 1887 in the Austro-Hungarian Empire, arrived in Newark in 1907, he saw horses everywhere, even pulling buses full of people. There were no radios or refrigerators, movies or vacuum cleaners, television or automatic washing machines. Only the rich had telephones. But he lived long enough to drive a car down superhighways while Sputnik beeped overhead. He observed more changes than he could have ever dreamed of—and so have we in our lifetimes.

One important change, which we take for granted, is that high culture became accessible to ordinary people through the expansion of a system of free public libraries that began at the end of the nineteenth century.

Books had arrived in the English colonies with the earliest settlers on the *Mayflower*, a number of men had private libraries in their houses, and university libraries served students. As early as 1731, Benjamin Franklin founded a public subscription (not free) library in Philadelphia, with similar institutions arising in Boston; Charleston, South Carolina; Newport, Rhode Island; and New York. These libraries already had some books appropriate for children on their shelves, including classics like *Aesops' Fables* (1484), *The Arabian Nights* (available in English by 1712), and *Mother Goose* (translated from the French around 1729). As time went on, books like *Alice in Wonderland* (1865), *Little Women* (1868), and *The Adventures of Tom Sawyer* (1876) joined them.

However, most books for children written before the twentieth century were either religious like *Pilgrim's Progress* (1678) or didactic like *The Book of Courtesye* (1497). The latter book, from the great English printer William Caxton, described how a well-bred English child ought to behave. In addition, many of the books, such as *Robinson Crusoe* (1719–20), had originally been published for adults; although children read them, they skipped the dull and difficult parts, and special children's editions expurgated material deemed inappropriate for young readers.

The first publishers were either printers like Caxton or booksellers like John Newbery (1713–67), who was one of the first to publish books especially designed for children. (The Newbery Medal—for the best children's book of the year written by an American—is named after him. It is awarded by the American Library Association.)

British illustrators like Walter Crane, Kate Greenaway, and Randolph Caldecott emerged in the nineteenth century with their drawings of cheerful people, flowers, action scenes, and animals. Advances in printing made color drawings possible. (The Caldecott Medal—for the best illustrated book of the year—is named for Randolph Caldecott and bears a reproduction of a drawing by him. This medal is also awarded by the American Library Association. Its winner and the winner of the Newbery Medal are both chosen at the association's midwinter meeting.)

Still, with some exceptions, there was a quaintness and unreality in many of these books, which tended to portray childhood as a universally happy time and gave children sentimental tales about fairies and elves.

It is perhaps significant that 1900 saw the publication of *The Tale of Peter Rabbit*, the story of a mischievous bunny remarkably like a real child. This was the same year Sigmund Freud's *The Interpretation of Dreams* was published in Vienna, heralding a new century with exciting ideas in psychology, education, and child development.

The public library system continued to expand, and by 1900 more than nine thousand libraries could be found around the country in rural and urban areas. Some libraries began to open children's rooms, and elementary and secondary schools also started to establish their own libraries. By 1915, the American Library Association had set up a school library division. It was not long before a number of librarians and other women (it was mostly women) decided children needed more books to enrich their minds and imaginations, books that were not textbooks, books that were not religious, trendy, or commercial. Dedicated librarians convinced publishers that a market was waiting for new books written and illustrated especially for children. The first trade children's book, or juvenile, department was opened in 1921 by Louise Seaman at Macmillan. This marked the beginning of modern children's trade book publishing, which set the standards for the books still being published today.

A few male publishers, whose families owned the firms, put the children's book departments in offices at the back of their quarters and let the ladies publish all the books about bunny rabbits they desired. At other houses, children's books like Felix Salten's *Bambi* (1928) were published by the adult department. It soon became clear the "bunny books" were profitable, and juvenile departments opened at other firms.

Working in harmony with professional librarians like Anne Carroll Moore of the New York Public Library, the editors and librarians had high standards. Seaman of Macmillan, May Massee of Doubleday and Viking, and others wanted to publish literary, intelligent, and truthful books that would appeal to all children. They wanted the best artists to illustrate them. The librarians wanted the same things, and 95 percent of the juvenile books were sold to school and public libraries. Devoted to children's literature, the *Horn Book Magazine* began publication in Boston in 1921 with Bertha Mahoney as editor. And in 1929, the first children's book club, the Junior Literary Guild, began to send selected books to children all over the country.

In those days, most people in positions of power in the United States were white, Anglo-Saxon, Protestant, and upper middle-class. Since the librarians (and the publishers) were of similar background, the books they published were largely about and for middle-class children and their concerns. Many of the most highly regarded titles, such as *Wind in the Willows*, *The Story of Doctor Dolittle*, and *Winnie the Pooh*, came from England. In spite of their origin, these books transcended class boundaries. Of universal interest, with unforgettable characters, settings, and ideas, they appealed to all children, not only in the United States but around the world—which is what the best books do.

Talented people have long flocked to and from the United States to create new lives or to escape political troubles. Writers and artists like Wanda Gag from Czechoslovakia; Kate Seredy from Hungary; and Ludwig Bemelmans from Austria added a continental flavor to the predominantly Anglo-Saxon menu of books. William Pène du Bois's father was an American artist who moved to France, where Pène du Bois was educated. This was the golden age of children's books, which many say began in the United States in 1929 with the publication of a hopeful tale born on the eve of the Great Depression, *Millions of Cats* by Wanda Gag.

Kate Seredy, who had fallen on hard times in the 1970s, declared in a letter to her publisher that her books—and those of other juvenile writers—had kept the Viking Press afloat during the Depression. This was true, and Thomas Guinzburg, the owner of Viking, acknowledged it by sending her an advance on her royalties to help her.

To their amazement, publishers had found that juvenile books sold well even though jobs were scarce, people were standing in bread lines, and the banks were bankrupt. It was not only books. All forms of entertainment—especially the movies—did well as people looked for ways to forget their economic woes and the horrors of World War II. In the 1940s Walt Disney movies thrilled families with versions of favorite children's books and stories, such as *Pinocchio* by Carlo Collodi and *Ferdinand*, a pacifist tale about a bull, by Robert Lawson.

Commercial lines of books—the ancestors of today's mass

market titles—for children were also available. Literary quality took second place to action-packed, often garish, stories in the form of the dime novel or series books like the Horatio Alger stories with stereotyped characters and cliffhangers at the end of every chapter.

The most enduring and successful "fiction factory" was that of Edward Stratemeyer, who, as owner of what became known as the Stratemeyer Syndicate, published hundreds of books from Tom Swift to the Hardy Boys series under a variety of pseudonyms around the turn of the century and later. Howard R. Garis and his wife, Lillian, wrote most of the Tom Swift and Bobbsey Twins books—he could write a book every eight or ten days. Leslie McFarlane, who used the pseudonym Franklin W. Dixon, wrote most of the original Hardy Boys books.

When Stratemeyer's daughter, Harriet, protested that her father wasn't publishing books for girls, he said, "Girls don't read." Harriet proved him wrong by starting the Nancy Drew line of mysteries, which were written by Mildred Wirt Benson under the pseudonym Carolyn Keene. Benson said in a National Public Radio interview in 1993 that Nancy was perfect, a fantasy creation who never made a mistake or had any flaws. Nancy Drew is still going strong, as are other, newer lines of series books, mostly in paperback editions. The stock complaint now is that boys don't read!

As the century grew older, children had access to comic books (*Superman* was born in 1936), radio, movies, television, video games, and computers. When each new temptation to put down a book arose, so did dire predictions about the death of high-quality books for children. Yet juvenile publishing, though it has changed a great deal from the days of Louise Seaman, remains a strong and vital industry.

In the first half of the twentieth century, the editors at the major publishing houses founded a reading empire that is to be envied. As the editorial staffs grew, young women joined them straight from college, without becoming librarians first. The editors gave the youngest children picture books with first-rate artwork, in black and white and in color. Many of these are still on the shelves of libraries. Fiction for older children, including marvelous books of folk and fairy tales, opened up the world and gave readers an enviable vocabulary. Books satisfied curious children by providing accurate and up-to-date information about science, history, and other nonfiction topics. The first winner of the Newbery Award, in 1922, was *The Story of Mankind* by Hendrik van Loon, a writer born in the Netherlands. For the first time ever, thanks to the free public library system in the United States, nearly all children had access to books of poetry, humor, fantasy, and realistic fiction as well as up-to-date nonfiction written especially for them.

This trend continued to the end of the century. By the year 2001, no longer was the juvenile publishing field dominated by white middle-class women. Editors actively sought out writers from minority groups, and the 1970s saw a flowering of multicultural literature. Children's book writers and editors today come from many classes, races, religions, sexual preferences, and national backgrounds. Old taboos about sexual activity, street language, and controversial subject matter began to fade in the 1960s, though censorship and informed concern about what is appropriate for children remained alive.

However, the most serious threat to the continuation of the library-centered tradition was the discovery that children's books made money, or "Children's Books Mean Business," a slogan from the 1980s. Large corporations bought and absorbed small publishing houses; the family firms nearly became extinct. As Craig Virden, president and publisher of juvenile hardcovers and paperbacks at Bantam Doubleday Dell said ruefully in *Publishers Weekly*, "Forget quaint and old-fashioned children's book publishing. 'Bunny eat bunny' has become dog eat dog." The profits and prestige have improved, so men head many children's departments today and must answer to executives who hold M.B.A.s, not degrees in the liberal arts.

We all know about the many babies born since 1990, a peak year for births. Parents—and grandparents—eagerly buy books for children; schools emphasize reading. Yet, paradoxically, in the 1990s many writers began to wonder whether they had chosen the right career as publishing houses reduced their lists, cut back on staff, and shut the doors to unsolicited manuscripts. Some venerable houses even vanished.

In spite of the changes, this is an excellent time to be a writer for children if you cast off old ideas. A time of transition is never easy, but neither is it a disaster. It is a time to take up the challenge of new markets and new ways of doing things.

2

Multiplying Like, Well, Rabbits

✦

THE GROWTH OF PAPERBACK BOOKS
FOR CHILDREN

*I'd rather be a failure at something I enjoy
than be a success at something I hate.* —*George Burns*

I t was summer, and I was eleven, walking past a candy store on Main Street. I glanced in the window and saw something new: a rack of thick paperback books. One book was titled *A Wonder Book for Boys and Girls*, and the other was *Tanglewood Tales for Girls and Boys*; both were by Nathaniel Hawthorne. I couldn't believe the phrase "for girls and boys" was on a book cover in a candy store! The books cost twenty-five cents each. I didn't know who Hawthorne was, but I knew I could afford to buy those books of Greek myths from the money I'd made collecting soda bottles for the deposit. It wasn't long before I owned the books and was reading them over and over. They were the first books I ever bought for myself.

Many Americans can remember a time when books—whether for adults or children—were almost exclusively published in expensive hardcover editions, available for sale only in some three thousand bookstores nationwide, most of them in cities. Books were treasured possessions in some families, status symbols in others. But many homes had no books at all, not even a Bible. At the time of the Great Depression, the only places to find good books to read were schools, libraries, and lending libraries, which were private "libraries" that rented books.

A few attempts had been made to introduce paperbound editions to American readers, but they had failed. Although he was not alone in wanting to change this state of affairs, Ian Ballantine was probably the most innovative, the most enthusiastic, and the most loved of a new breed that successfully brought paperback books into American life. As Irwyn Applebaum of what was then known as Bantam Doubleday Dell (now Random House) said at Ballantine's memorial service in 1995, "Ian was the Mad Hatter who hopped [sic] away [from the literary tea] and started up the wild, wonderful mass-market paperback party, invited everybody—absolutely everybody—to join in, and made it his lifelong mission to keep it roaring."

Around the same time that Ballantine began to import the English line of Penguin paperbacks into the United States, Pocket Books issued its first ten reprints of popular books, making it the first modern American paperback publisher. Booksellers and readers greeted the two new lines, which complemented each other, with enthusiasm, so much so that people began to call all paperbacks "pocket books."

In 1943 George Delacorte, founder of Dell Publishing, added mysteries, westerns, and romances to his successful lines of magazines and comic books. Dell and the other magazine publishers had unparalleled direct distribution into the magazine market: about one hundred thousand candy stores, newsstands, drugstores, general stores—outlets found in the smallest of towns and the most far-flung places.

Ballantine was ready to fight it out with Pocket and Dell for leadership in the American market. He had signed a distribution contract with the Curtis Publishing Corporation, publishers of two of the most popular magazines in the country, the *Ladies' Home Journal* and the *Saturday Evening Post*. But Allen Lane, the British publisher of Penguin, was aghast. He did not want Penguin Books in outlets other than bookstores (a Penguin practice that was true until recently), he disliked the idea of illustrated covers (the original Penguins did not have art on the covers), and he was afraid the line would lose its British character.

Ballantine left Penguin, which continued with a new staff. Eventually the staff left, too, for reasons similar to Ballantine's, and founded New American Library. As president of Bantam, where he worked with Oscar Dystel, the cofounder, Ballantine was able to prove that packaging was as important as distribution. The first twenty books Ballantine published under the Bantam imprint appeared in November 1945, with printings of 200,000 each. He designed a rack for paperbacks, then went one step farther and *gave* the rack to merchants to display Bantam Books.

Under Ballantine and Dystel, Bantam also developed a separate sales force that sold to independent trade bookstores (there were almost no chains then). This was the first time mass-market paperbacks were sold from trade bookstores. Even before the merger in 1998 with Random House, Bantam, combined with Doubleday and Dell, was the largest paperback publisher in the United States, followed by Pocket Books.

Successful as Bantam was, Ballantine was dissatisfied. Always the innovator, he proposed some startling new ideas to the board of directors. When they turned down the ideas, he left Bantam and founded Ballantine Books in 1952.

As the science-fiction writer Robert Silverberg has said, "Writers don't consider publishers a lovable life-form." But, he went on to say about Ballantine, "he made us prosperous . . . he spread joy as well as dollars among us." Ballantine understood that writers needed economic security while writing, which is why advances are offered: to give the writer the time to write. Ballantine offered writers big advances, $5,000 per book, which could support a family quite nicely in the 1950s. His most helpful idea for writers was to sign up the rights simultaneously for books in hardcover and paper, known as a hard/soft deal. This effectively doubled the writer's income, because he could collect the full royalty on the paperback instead of splitting the income from a mass-market paperback sale with his hardcover publisher.

Ballantine was far ahead of his time. It was not until 1966 that Dell set up a hardcover line, Delacorte Press, and signed "hard/soft deals" with major writers like James Jones and Irwin Shaw. Although more publishers offer hard/soft deals these days, it is still not the norm.

Where do paperback books for children fit into this story? The adult paperbacks are, in effect, the parents of the juvenile lines. It was natural, once adult paperbacks were developed and established, for the business practice to spill over into the juvenile world. The paperback revolution in children's books could begin.

In the 1960s, only a few of the principal hardcover publishers had trade paperback lines, adult and some juvenile. Trade paperbacks are usually facsimiles—with card stock covers—of the hardbound editions. Sometimes the trim and type sizes are different, but that's for technical reasons. Viking had the Seafarer line, Harper's had Trophy, and Penguin had Puffin. Trade paperbacks were sold primarily through bookstores and did not have the same distribution as mass-market paperbacks.

In 1965, encouraged by the high sales of comic books, Helen Meyer, president of Dell, believed its magazine distribution system could handle children's books as well. She was right. A year later, under George Nicholson, Dell began its Yearling line of children's books, with such titles as *Charlotte's Web* by E. B. White and *Johnny Tremain*, a Newbery Medal book, by Esther Forbes. Dell had already launched the Laurel-Leaf imprint, which specialized in young adult titles.

Yearling Books were what is known as digest-sized trade paperbacks as far as quality went (except for the paper), but since they were sold by the paperback sales force, not the trade reps, they were considered mass market. Yearling Books never penetrated the mass market the way adult paperbacks did, but they did find their way into those bookstores that didn't have a bias against children's books or paperback books as many upscale stores did. The same was true for Laurel-Leaf, which were rack-sized editions and looked like adult books.

Dell and other mass-market paperback houses like Pocket Books and Avon Books managed to get juvenile paperbacks into more places than traditional hardcover sales strategies could. Hardcover houses with trade paper lines were happy to sell reprint rights to mass-market lines, splitting the advances and royalties with authors.

In the 1970s, publishers (and the rest of the country) were in deep financial trouble. Inflation was endemic because of the OPEC oil embargo, the end of the Vietnam War, and the many costly social programs of the Johnson administration. Taxpayers tightened local purses, salaries were frozen, yet prices kept going up. Juvenile book publishers had to take a different course, find new markets, if they were to survive. The fare served at the literary teas in the schools and libraries—which now made up about 65 percent of the market—simply was no longer substantial enough to keep publishers and writers healthy. Publishers took some cues from the hardcover mass-market houses like Random House and began to offer novelty books, such as pop-ups, to the stores.

In the 1970s, the chain bookstores like Waldenbooks and

Brentano's in the malls, unlike the independent store on Main Street, offered anonymity to children, who were clutching their own money, whether from allowances or jobs. The salespeople did not hover, nor did they know their young customers, who were free to buy what they liked, not what their parents dictated. The children and teenagers bought books like *Are You There, God? It's Me, Margaret* by Judy Blume and S. E. Hinton's *The Outsiders*.

Ron Buehl, who had replaced George Nicholson at Dell, seemed to have a bottomless checkbook in the early 1970s, and he astutely paid the highest advances at the time for paperback rights. Shock waves reverberated around the industry when word came that Dell had paid William Morrow and Company $1 million for the license to reprint eighteen titles by Beverly Cleary for seven years. Hardcover houses were grateful for the infusion of cash, but they began to lose some of their best-selling writers, who discovered how lucrative it was to close a hard/soft deal with a publisher that had its own mass-market paperback line. A book would be published in hardcover by Delacorte, for example, then in paperback by Yearling or Laurel-Leaf.

The 1970s also saw the rise of book producers, or packagers, like Cloverdale Press (founded by Dan and Jeff Weiss). Packagers had been around for a long time, but Cloverdale specialized in young adult paperback series—the hottest market at the time. Cloverdale astonished traditional publishers by creating Sweet Dreams, a romance series, which became number one on B. Dalton's best-seller list in 1982. The 1970s had seen the heyday of the problem novel, but in the 1980s these were not the books the kids in the malls wanted to read. Romance novels from Cloverdale and other packagers caused the demise of trade hi/lo books (high interest/low reading level) for reluctant readers, a genre that still survives in the school market. Nonfiction for teenagers had never sold well in paperback; it, too, died after ailing since the 1970s. Sales of literary novels and historical fiction in paper began to slacken. The mood of the country had become conservative and escapist. Juvenile paperbacks were well on the way to holding a fabulous mass-market feast of their own in the 1980s, especially since other companies like Pocket Books, Avon, New American Library, and Scholastic helped to feed the growing chain store markets with series that sold millions of copies.

By the 1990s, movie and TV tie-ins proliferated, with such successes as the *Teen-Age Mutant Ninja Turtles*, which went from a Saturday morning TV show to paperback, and Goosebumps, which went from a series of books by R. L. Stine to TV and the movies and racks in the supermarkets. Series came and went on TV and in the bookstores. Juvenile paperbacks were no longer simply inexpensive reprints of high-quality hardcover books. They had become the principal moneymakers for the corporations that now owned almost all of juvenile publishing. Some writers made more money than they had ever dreamed of. It was backbreaking to write book after book, as Ann M. Martin did to keep her successful Baby-Sitters Club series going, but the financial return was mind-boggling. Many writers longed to create a best-selling paperback series, but only a few were smash successes, like the Animorphs books by Katherine Applegate, which appeared at the end of the 1990s. Like all bonanzas, the rise of paperbacks in the bookstores was a mixed blessing, as we shall see later.

3

Mr. McGregor Buys a Suit

✦

JUVENILE PUBLISHING BECOMES
BIG BUSINESS

The future has a way of arriving unannounced.
—*George Will*

Most firms were privately held and paternalistic when I
started my publishing career in the 1960s; that is, they
were owned by families like the Doubledays and the Scribners,
who did not open their accounts to public scrutiny, because the
firms were not on the stock exchange. The owners worked on the
premises, knew the staff personally, and often came by to visit the
various departments. At the old Viking Press, one such owner,
Thomas Guinzburg, would send champagne to the juvenile department whenever something needed to be celebrated, such as
winning a major award. The atmosphere was professional, the
feeling collegial.

Anyone can become a publisher, which used to mean "owner."

The pattern is that a man, like Henry Holt, or a woman, like Mary Roberts Rinehart, would begin a publishing house and use his or her name. Later they might merge and pick up another partner, like Winston. In spite of the hyphens or ampersands, the firms were still private and "family" owned, passing down from founder to heirs. A few major corporations are still privately held, but that is the exception.

Bennett Cerf and Donald Klopfer made publishing history in 1925 when they bought the Modern Library, hardcover reprints of classics, from Boni & Liveright, one of the most distinguished literary houses at that time. Two years later Cerf and Klopfer established Random House. In 1960 Cerf became the first of the publishers to go cosmodemonic (as per Henry Miller, who coined the name Cosmodemonic for the firm where he worked as a young man), with his purchase of Knopf (including Vintage Paperbacks), Beginner Books, I. W. Singer, then Pantheon. RCA bought it all in 1966 and sold it to S. I. Newhouse and Donald Newhouse in 1980. But that's history, because eighteen years later Random House was sold to the same people who own Bantam Doubleday Dell, the Bertlesmann Corporation based in Germany.

Meanwhile, the 1960s saw other significant mergers take place. The Macmillan Company was absorbed into a large corporation: Crowell Collier Macmillan. New antitrust laws permitted the joining of many different companies into one corporation, or conglomerate, as long as the companies were in related industries.

Employees of the old Macmillan (publishers of *Gone with the Wind* and *The Collected Poems of W. B. Yeats* and *A Snowy Day* by Ezra Jack Keats) went into shock when they were forced to move from their fusty, historic offices in Greenwich Village into a new (and air-conditioned) office building at Fifty-third Street and Third Avenue in New York. Employees felt they were working inside a giant machine, and the spirit of rebellion was in the air. It was the 1960s, after all.

Collier's magazine and encyclopedia had disappeared by then, but the name was preserved in the Collier line of trade paperbacks and in a new juvenile line called Crowell-Collier Press, dedicated to publishing curriculum-related nonfiction for school and public libraries, or the "institutional market." President Lyndon B. Johnson's Great Society plans included Title II, a government program, which made $100 million available for creating or improving school libraries. Schools that had never had a library could start one with federal help, and existing libraries could buy new books. Always an important market, libraries became even more influential and demanded nonfiction especially. The usual print run for a Crowell-Collier Press book was 15,000. Many new and established writers and illustrators did books for this growing market. Susan Jeffers, for example, illustrated one of her first books for Crowell-Collier Press. Ben Bova and Jan Slepian also wrote for the line.

At that time, the Macmillan trade juvenile department was headed by Susan Carr Hirschmann, who had served her publishing apprenticeship under the great editor at Harper's, Ursula Nordstrom. Crowell-Collier Press and Macmillan juvenile had different

editorial staffs and goals, but they shared many of the design, production, and marketing facilities, and both lines prospered.

Like a surreal technological garden, Third Avenue was growing high rises, because the old elevated railway, the El, had recently been torn down, bringing light, air, and relative quiet back
to the broad street. As time went on, to save money on rent, more
publishers moved east of Madison Avenue, with Dell and Dial the
farthest, on Second Avenue near the United Nations. Young editors often worked at one house, then went to another to further
their careers, and finally ended up at a third, where they stayed for
the rest of their lives. It seemed that everyone knew everyone else
and that the houses where one worked were like so many alma
maters. One observed certain mores, such as not raiding authors
edited by acquaintances. *Raiding* meant "stealing," and it was
frowned upon as much as actual theft was.

No major trend happens overnight. What happened to the
"gentleman's (or lady's) profession" of publishing happened to
other corporations much earlier primarily because publishing was
never a Big Money business like steel, banking, or the movies.
"Children's books stay straight," the illustrator Donald Carrick
said in the 1960s, "because there's no money in it." Gertrude P.
Schafer, the managing editor with whom I worked at Viking, put
it another way: "It's a nickel-and-dime business," she told me, by
which she meant every nickel counted. Salaries were low, but that
was the price one paid for what economists call high "psychic income"—deriving pleasure in one's work.

In the 1970s, though, children's publishing felt the pinch.

After the Vietnam War ended, Title II dried up, and we were in the midst of "stagflation": low economic growth accompanied by high prices. The prices of everything, including paper, skyrocketed; the words *cash flow* came into common parlance, because the cash was hardly flowing at all; interest rates were too high; salaries were frozen by President Richard M. Nixon's economic policies. The small, private publishers were in serious financial trouble.

Media corporations bought and sold publishers like herring. CBS bought Little, Brown and later sold it to Time-Warner; Gulf + Western bought Simon & Schuster, then sold it to Paramount. The publishing executives touted an exciting concept dubbed *synergy*. It would be more profitable, they said, to publish the books that would become blockbuster movies, and thereby save money since the same firm—albeit a different division—would already own the performance rights. Foreign publishers also began to buy American publishers. Penguin (English) bought Viking, Holtzbrinck (German) bought Holt, and Collins (English) bought Harper's.

For the most part, children's books, still in the back rooms, remained a cottage industry under the corporate roof, and the editor in chief was still the boss of her or his department. She approved the purchases of manuscripts she and her editors discovered, and she supervised the work of the library promotion department. She selected the art to go on the catalog cover, for example, and decided which book should get a poster. The library promotion department carried out her wishes.

We in the children's book field had always thought that our

work was important and profitable enough, and we suffered through all the jokes about bunny rabbit books. The prestige was in the front office with the "grown-ups," but freedom and happiness was in the back, exactly as Beatrix Potter's Tom Kitten had discovered when he was banned from his mother's tea party. Whenever a famous writer or an occasional celebrity was in the building, the news hit the grapevine. Like children during their parents' cocktail party, we'd sneak peeks at Mary Hemingway or William Saroyan or Willie Mays or Saul Bellow or Nadine Gordimer. But in the back room, we got to *talk* to people like Don Freeman and Robert Burch and Joan Aiken and Ossie Davis. They were at the children's table with us, and we were delighted to be in their company.

Publishing is labor-intensive. Acquiring, editing, designing, producing, marketing a number of new books every year require that each one be handled by many people during the process between submission of a manuscript and selling a finished book. It is not the same as producing, say, cans of soda, which are identical, year after year. As the 1970s trudged on, book paper got flimsier, the full cloth binding just about disappeared, and raises were nonexistent. Although sales to the paperback reprint houses saved many a hardcover children's line, writers began to find that their success was being measured first by whether the rights were sold and second by how many copies "went out the door."

After Ronald Reagan was elected president in 1980, the antitrust and tax laws were rewritten. Any company could pretty much buy any other, whether it was in a related industry or not.

Underpaid workers who had felt secure began to find they were "redundant." The buzzword among the M.B.A.s was *productivity*, which meant "downsizing" and being "lean and mean." This thinking affected all industries, not only publishing.

After years of editors and sales reps telling booksellers that children's books could be profitable, the penny dropped. Booksellers who hadn't paid attention before heard the message: "Children's Books Mean Business." At annual meetings of the American Booksellers Association in the mid-1980s, owners and salespeople heard about the quantities of children's books being sold, especially backlist books. At almost the same moment, Collins Publishers bought the venerable house of Harper's and renamed it HarperCollins; the Australian publishing magnate Rupert Murdoch owns about a third of the stock.

Children's publishers had always made most of their profits from the backlists. The *frontlist* is the current group of books published by a house. The *backlist* contains all the books published in previous seasons to which the publisher still holds the rights. "Plant costs" (such as the cost of setting type or making color plates) had been paid for, and second, third, and twenty-ninth printings were cheaper than first printings. All the traditional houses had important backlists, but Harper's may have had the most impressive of all. This is a bit fanciful, of course, but I believe that when the new HarperCollins management people saw how the Harper juvenile backlist brought in money, they realized that children's books indeed meant business. Harper's "cash cows" like *Charlotte's Web* and Laura Ingalls Wilder's Little House books—a mere sample of the feast—sped into and out of stores and libraries. "Publish more books," the M.B.A.s said! "This is a piece of cake."

And that spelled the end of traditional hardcover publishing as it had been in so many houses. Business majors who had no feeling for the liberal arts began to tell editors in chief what to publish. One lost her job, she told me, because the executives said she didn't publish enough best-sellers! The library promotion department became the library marketing department, and then simply "marketing." Gradually, the people who knew and loved books, including editors, lost power to people who probably would have been just as happy selling underwear.

Meanwhile, one publishing company after another began to merge (or be submerged) at a dizzying rate. In its March 17, 1997, issue, the *Nation* published a chart of the "octopoly," the eight major corporations that made up what the magazine called "The Media Nation." It seemed even more certain that all the major publishers would eventually be joined into the Cosmodemonic Media Corp. We are not far from that day, since at this writing only five major trade publishers from the *Nation* list remain, with most of the traditional juvenile imprints under their control.

This has had serious repercussions for the writers of children's books since many imprints either have been moved to new homes or have vanished entirely. Imprints are individual publishing departments within a larger company. Many were once publishing houses themselves. In 1994 Simon & Schuster bought Macmillan, including the juvenile books, which had fallen on hard times after the mysterious death of Robert Maxwell, the British tycoon who owned it. It seemed that Macmillan had no sooner bought a number of private publishing companies (Atheneum, Bradbury Press, Scribners, Margaret McElderry Books) when they were sold and ended up as part of Simon & Schuster or were closed down, as in the case of Bradbury, the Scribner juvenile department, and the Atheneum adult trade department. The loss of an imprint is a loss of a market for manuscripts.

Paramount owned Simon & Schuster, but in 1995 Viacom purchased Paramount. By the year 2000, Viacom had achieved its announced intention to sell all of its publishing businesses other than the Consumer Group (which had briefly been called Paramount Publishing), which publishes trade books, many of them best-sellers. Viacom is on the way to becoming, said Sumner M. Redstone, chairman of the board and chief executive officer, in a letter to stockholders, "*the* preeminent software-driven entertainment company in the world." Given that Viacom owns, in part or wholly, Blockbuster, MTV, Nickelodeon, Paramount Pictures, UPN, and Paramount Parks (among other entities), selling off its educational, reference, and professional book groups would enable Viacom to step "ahead boldly into a new era as a focused entertainment company." It also meant that several markets for nonfiction books shrank or vanished, including the Silver Burdett school library line.

When the Viking Penguin Putnam merger occurred in 1997, Cobblehill Press and Lodestar, at the Viking-Penguin group, "disappeared." In 1998, as already mentioned, the Bertlesmann Corporation bought Random House to add to its earlier acquisitions of Bantam, Doubleday, and Dell. Not much later, in 1999, HarperCollins bought the Hearst Group, a privately held company, which included Morrow Junior Books; Lothrop, Lee, and Shepard; Greenwillow Books; and Avon Books. The Harper children's book department moved to 1350 Avenue of the Americas, and the Morrow adult departments moved to the Harper Fifth Avenue office.

Writers found it mind-boggling to keep track of all the changes as publishers moved their offices, got rid of existing staff and hired new people, and had confusing policies about manuscript submissions. At some houses, each imprint has its own readers; at others, readers evaluate manuscripts for several departments.

The results of the consolidations have had other consequences for writers, agents, and publishing staff. The saddest is that imprints vanish, as with Bradbury Press, the original publisher of Judy Blume's *Are You There, God? It's Me, Margaret*. (Ironically, two former Macmillan employees, Richard Jackson and Bob Verrone, had founded Bradbury in the 1960s to escape corporate life!) All the nonfiction institution-oriented imprints at Simon & Schuster and Macmillan—Julian Messner, Dillon Press, Crestwood, Silver Burdett trade—became part of Macmillan Reference and were later sold to Pearson, which owned the Viking Penguin complex. All the imprints were later disbanded, contracts canceled, and backlists destroyed, meaning a significant loss of income to writers.

The principal difference between a cosmodemonic corporation and a small firm is that the big companies want huge profits in a hurry to please their stockholders. Andre Schiffrin, publisher of the New Press, noted in the *Nation* that after-tax profits of about 4 to 5 percent contented the owners of small trade houses. By contrast, the cosmodemonic firms are looking for profits of from 12 to 15 percent. They need new blockbuster books, including children's books, every year! The independent firms, which are in business for the long haul, can afford to be patient and will support and publish many books by a writer until she becomes established. Cosmodemonic will give you one or two chances to make it as a profitable writer. If you don't, you are dropped.

If an editor at a private firm (or at an old-style imprint at some major corporations) feels sure you'll make it eventually, you'll have the chance to write more books for that company. If your books are well received, you will become better known as you write more. Slowly (if not surely), your reputation will grow, and so will your sales. This is how it used to be done almost everywhere. A writer could survive by writing one book a year, every year, and by the time ten had been published, he could probably afford to live on the income from his royalties and become a full-time writer. This is rarely so now. Back when Ian Ballantine paid writers advances of $5,000, children's book writers were getting advances of $750 to $1,500 per book. Some best-selling juvenile writers may do extremely well today, but most of the rest are earning between $1,500 and $10,000 a book.

Although this sounds grim, it is not the whole story. We may never return to the way things were once done, but writers will continue to get their books published, and we may be in the midst of a new era as exciting as that of the past, when anyone could start a publishing company and prosper. It is still possible. It is happening now.

4

What's Up, Doc?

✦

THE CHANGING MARKETPLACE

Teaching kids to count is fine, but teaching them what counts is best. —*Bob Talbert*

The mergers and restructuring of the 1980s and 1990s shrank the literary, library-oriented, juvenile hardcover market. With the vanishing of so many imprints, it became harder for writers to get their work published at a traditional house. On the other hand, the bookstore market was hopping, especially with mass-market children's books. One reason: We are in the midst of a baby boom louder than the one after World War II.

Businesses pay serious attention to demographics, and writers, too, must be aware of how the young population is "aging" and tailor their books appropriately. If you live in a small town or suburb, you already know of the need for new or expanded schools. The wedge of readers born since around 1990 is determining which markets publishers are most eager to reach. A U.S. Department of

Education statistical projection predicts that the total enrollment of children from kindergarten to the twelfth grade will be 54.2 million students by 2003, which is more than the 51.3 million students in 1971 during the post-World War II baby boom. About 38 million will be in kindergarten through the eighth grade, and about 16 million in secondary school. That is a lot of children and teenagers! They will need a lot of books—*new* books!

A high proportion of these children have parents who are college educated and upwardly mobile. Composed of all races and ethnic backgrounds, this group of parents has high expectations for its children. Knowing that reading is important for material success, parents begin to read to their children as soon as they're born, if not before. They want their children to attend the best schools—often private or parochial—and do well on tests. The grandparents of these children feel the same way. In a survey commissioned by the American Association of Retired Persons, published in the spring of 2000, 60 percent of the grandparents surveyed listed books as their first choice of gifts for their grandchildren; only 38 percent bought toys. These middle-class parents and grandparents, as well as aunts, uncles, and other relations, all buy children's books, beginning with board books for the cradle set, picture books for the slightly older children, and then paperback fiction and some hardcover nonfiction.

So even though publishing has become more competitive, it has a large and diverse market to serve, which is good for writers. More books are being published. On the other hand, the big numbers are not in the traditional hardcover trade books (except for some picture books) for a number of reasons, one of which is that most parents and many booksellers are in the dark about children's literature, especially contemporary books. Sales are highest in mass market, which includes not only paperbacks but the "low end" (inexpensive books) of hardcover publishing. Dr. Seuss and Richard Scarry were among the wealthiest of writers for children.

After children's publishers bragged to American booksellers that "children's books mean business," and the publishing executives saw it was true, bookstores began to take children's books seriously—but only in the categories they felt they could sell. And there's the rub. There's little room for eccentricity of taste or titles that don't sell in large numbers. While many of the clerks in the adult departments are first-rate, many in the children's book area are not educated about their stock.

The independent bookstore still survives in a form not too different from that shown in old movies and television programs. The owners of independent stores are just that: independent. They decide what to stock, depending on their knowledge of the local market. They read books and are known for their ability to recommend, or "hand sell," titles they admire. More than a few times, they have been instrumental in propelling books to the best-seller lists.

Tempting and cheaper though it may be to order books from on-line sources or to sip coffee and then buy your book at a major chain bookstore, if you are a writer, your best friend may be the struggling owner of your local bookstore—especially if it's a children's-only shop. Make friends with the staff and buy books there. Otherwise, the independent bookstore may one day exist only in the fantasies of book lovers, and it will be even harder to get into print.

The major bookstore chains like Barnes & Noble, the largest chain, and Borders, the second largest, have come to dominate the bookselling scene, dwarfing even the old chains like Doubleday, Brentano's, and B. Dalton. Venerable and respected stores all over the United States have closed their doors for good or been submerged; Waldenbooks, for example, is now part of Borders.

It is frightening to contemplate the carnage that can occur when a major chain comes on the scene, even in a place as densely populated with bookstores as Manhattan. The chains offer discounts, thousands of books and related merchandise, special programs, comfortable places to sit and read, and cafés. Store after store—many of them legendary and successful, once beloved by readers and writers—has been forced out of business because it could not compete with the high-volume chain stores.

This trend affects publishers and writers alike. The publishers strive to produce books the national chains will buy. If the buyers for these chains, known as national accounts, turn down an individual title or declare lack of interest in a category, the book is in trouble. In March 1998, the American Booksellers Association (ABA) filed an antitrust lawsuit in the U.S. District Court for the Northern District of California against Barnes & Noble and Borders. The suit on behalf of the ABA and more than twenty independent bookstores alleges that these large national chain stores are using their clout with publishers to obtain secret and illegal deals and preferential treatment such as deep discounts not available to the independent booksellers. One of the plaintiffs, Clark Kepler, owner of Kepler's Books & Magazines in Menlo Park, California, said: "This fight is about preserving what America is able to read. A network of healthy independent bookstores spurs publishers to produce a diversity of literature and to take risks with authors who are of less commercial but greater critical appeal."

Who doesn't like the convenience of buying books online? I wonder how many people are browsing at a local bookstore, then buying from Amazon.com, which claims an inventory of 2.5 million titles? Books Online from Bertelsmann offers books in major languages with discounts competitive with Amazon.com and Barnes & Noble on-line, which stocks 350,000 titles. Bertelsmann also operates Boulevard Online, an electronic bookstore based in Germany.

Not to be outdone, many independent stores have set up Web sites of their own; it's just as easy to order from down the street as from other on-line sources. And when it made its debut in the fall of 2000, the American Booksellers Association Book Sense (www.BookSense.com) marketing program featured a database of more than 2 million titles, which can be ordered on-line, offered by independent bookstores.

Another major influence on book sales remains the giant book wholesalers, such as Baker and Taylor and Ingram, which order copies in advance of publication and hold them ready to ship to libraries and bookstores at a moment's notice. If the rate of movement (ROM) of a title is energetic, the wholesaler will keep ordering stock. On the other hand, if the ROM is lethargic, the wholesaler will not order more copies, and the ROM will slow down and even stop.

Publishers, national accounts, and wholesalers monitor the ROMs of all titles. A best-seller might fly out of the warehouses and stores at the rate of 10,000 copies a week. Or 800 copies of a new children's novel may be ordered by a wholesaler, and then, if sales are not brisk, never reordered. At some publishers, a ROM under, say, 250 hardcover copies a month guarantees the book will be declared "out of stock" (OS) as soon as the supply is exhausted.

"Out of stock" is not the same as "out of print" (OP), though it can seem that way to the writer and even the bookseller. I learned about this when my sister-in-law, Jackie, went to a local small-town bookstore in 1981 to buy a copy of *The New York Kids Book*, which had been published by Doubleday in the fall of 1979. Unlike most books for children, this one had been reviewed by the *New York Times*, *New York* magazine, and other media, including newspapers and TV. Along with seven other writers, I'd been a contributing editor to this book and knew it intimately, to say the least. Jackie told me the clerk had looked it up "on the computer" and discovered it was "out of print." I called our editor at Doubleday, and she assured me copies were in the Doubleday warehouse. But the *wholesaler* had not reordered after the initial copies had sold out, and the bookstore computer told the owner the book was out of stock—at the wholesaler! Jackie was able to buy a copy directly from Doubleday, but, regrettably, that was not enough of a market to keep the book *in print* for long.

The good news for writers of children's books is that the major chains have large, well-stocked, and inviting children's book departments. Decorated with colorful art showing favorite characters from children's books, the areas are designed so that as soon as customers get close they will see the merchandise (dolls and the like) that goes with certain titles. Unfortunately, the emphasis on toys contributes to the feeling that the department is for the youngest of children. Nannies and babies in strollers find it's a comfortable place to meet other nannies and babies, especially in inclement weather.

Past the area dedicated to the youngest readers is shelf after shelf of paperback fiction, including classics and all the Newbery Medal books in print. The series readers, many of whom like to buy by number instead of title, will find the latest additions for their collections. Dotted around the area are dumps, or cardboard display units, featuring the most popular current series, seasonal promotions, movie and TV tie-ins, new series, or a variety of titles of other books of special interest. Bookstores also stock some non-fiction. The likeliest to be found have catchy titles and lavish illustrations. It seems as if all young needs can be satisfied here, except for new hardcover fiction for young readers, which traditionally has sold poorly in bookstores.

If a teenager sets foot in this department, he might find the paperback books for his age group in a corner, embarrassingly close to the nonfiction adult titles relating to breast-feeding and other aspects of child rearing. This is policy at some chains, and the staff is not free to change it. A good independent bookseller is sensitive to her clientele and segregates the books for small children; books for teen readers are in a rack strategically placed next to the novels in the *adult* section of the store.

If the major chains dominate the bookstore world, how can you, the writer, increase the chances of having your book sold at a chain? People unversed in the children's book field think creating a doll or other toy to accompany a book is a great idea. Well, yes it is, but it is illegal for someone to create a doll based on an existing character in a book without permission, or a license, from the owner. Characters are considered intellectual property, and their use is regulated through licensing.

Before the 1980s, only the most famous of juvenile trade book characters—Raggedy Ann and Andy, Corduroy, Madeline, Pippi Longstocking—had dolls developed in their likenesses. The rule was—and remains—that "merchandise" will sell to the public only when a character is already well established and popular, which was the case with mass-market characters like Snoopy and Mickey Mouse but not with trade book characters, even the most beloved. The number of people who recognized these characters was too small, it was believed.

A glance at the shelves at the bookstore demonstrates how this policy has changed. Publishers dived into their backlists and, sometimes with the help of outside book producers, found all kinds of ingenious ways to present merchandise featuring what are known as "licensed characters" to accompany certain books. Clifford the Big Red Dog, the Wild Thing (from Maurice Sendak's book *Where the Wild Things Are*), and many others are on the shelves now. But the old rule remains: The books must already be well known before their characters will be licensed.

On occasion, a toy may become so popular that a book or series of books (mass market) will be developed for it—like Barbie, who even has her own magazine. But it took Barbie a long time to reach printed form. For a good part of her life, she was just a toy! Therefore, if you have an idea for a toy and think it lends itself to books, think again. Publishers are conservative. They need to be sure the toy, the licensed character, is indeed popular before they will invest in books to accompany it. As always, they want to sell books, not toys; the manuscript comes first. If someone is willing to publish the book, the next step may come in regard to the toy. Keep in mind that publishers do not manufacture the toys themselves; they or the creators license the rights to others.

Near the merchandise books are a fair number of board, or concept, books for the youngest of children, babies and toddlers. Since these books are usually conceived in-house or by packagers, this is not a recommended path for a writer unless the writer is also an illustrator or knows an experienced, professional children's book artist who can carry out the idea. It is possible to "package" a simple eight-page book, offering text and art together. Since every possible concept has been done already—from counting to colors—the creator must supply a fresh and unique execution of old ideas, usually in a set of four books. Rosemary Wells did this brilliantly in her Max books, for example.

Novelty books, such as pop-ups, have also become favorites in bookstores. These require elaborate, *working* dummies, or mock-ups, for presenting to publishers. If you are able to do this yourself or to pay something like $10,000 to a paper engineer for a *professional* presentation, you can then send or take the material around yourself. Another possibility is to show your work to packagers, who have the resources to develop your ideas in return for a share of the proceeds.

If you are determined to do board or novelty books, be persistent and learn from your failures. Meeting editors, art directors, and packagers will give you exposure, and you may one day be invited to develop an idea for a publisher or packager. The American Book Producers Association, listed in the appendix, can help you find out which packagers specialize in concept and novelty books. Publishing people have traditionally been helpful. Once you have a list of editors, you'll find it will grow quickly through referrals.

The young writer who was mentioned in the preface, Gus, isn't sure he can succeed in the new world of publishing, by which he means support himself as a full-time writer. The chances are about the same as always. Writing for a living remains a risky undertaking. Few juvenile writers have ever earned enough to quit their day jobs.

It's no coincidence that so many published writers for children were married women, who had husbands to support them, or men who had wives who worked outside the home to supplement the family income. They could write a book a year for the library market and eventually break through to a comfortable living, sometimes surpassing their spouses' incomes. But if writers like

Gus have only one income from a day job and wish to support themselves solely by writing, they will have to hustle to find other work as freelance writers. Fortunately, the children's book field has grown, and opportunities for freelancers exist in new sorts of ventures.

The strong interest in children's books at all the bookstores—chain and independent—is great news for juvenile writers. People love children's books, and they are now available to more readers than ever. According to one bookseller, the Harry Potter books by J. K. Rowling have taught buyers about the wealth of reading material available only in hardcover, and her store is now stocking more hardcover fiction.

If this means a new trend will be established, let us give thanks to J. K. Rowling. As she knows, finding your book on sale in bookstores is a great boost to your career and to your determination to succeed as a writer.

PART II

✦

Foreground

5

Hop to It!

✦

WHERE TO FIND A PUBLISHER

*If a window of opportunity appears, don't pull down
the shade. —Tom Peters*

My friend Gus, the writer, was scratching his head. "On the one hand," he said to me, "the market has contracted. Then you say more opportunities exist than ever. Which is it?"

"Both statements are true," I answered. "Many of the traditional imprints no longer exist. On the other hand, adjustments have been made to counter the effects of the mergers among the cosmodemonic firms."

I went on to remind Gus that the children's book market has always been diverse and stratified. Today, it is more diverse than ever, which is good news for writers. Some publishers continue in the venerable traditions of the library-oriented market. Others aim at schools, bookstores, or even toy stores. Therefore, many children's book markets exist, and what is wrong for one may well be perfect for another.

Literary editors have had to learn to coexist with the business-minded executives and their new procedures. Other editors have been lucky enough to found imprints at kinder, gentler publishers of the old school. Some have established publishing companies of their own or gone into book producing. Many editors are working freelance for packagers or as consultants. Most important, though, for the writer is the rise of new publishers all over the country.

Understanding the different markets is a major step toward success as a writer for children. As a literary agent and a former editor, I've received thousands of manuscripts to consider for publication. Many looked as if they might be publishable, and they were read and either accepted or declined. (Editors never reject manuscripts; they decline them.) However, many submissions were clearly not right from the start; they were sent back unread in the enclosed SASE (self-addressed stamped envelope) or thrown away if no SASE had been enclosed. This was often not a reflection on the quality of the work but on the writer's failure to understand what a trade children's book was.

Traditional hardcover children's books, like Maurice Sendak's picture book *Where the Wild Things Are* and E. B. White's novel *Charlotte's Web*, are trade juveniles. One definition of a trade book is "a book sold in bookstores." Publishers like Viking; Harper-Collins; Farrar, Straus, & Giroux; and Little, Brown are in the trade book business.

As you've seen in the previous chapters, the primary destination for a trade juvenile (fiction or nonfiction) was not a bookstore but a school or public library (the institutional market). Thirty years ago, few hardcover trade books for children were sold in bookstores—about 95 percent went to libraries. It's been estimated that today only 50 percent of trade juveniles go to libraries.

Therefore, during the last twenty-five years juvenile trade houses began to publish books that would have a greater appeal in bookstores, books that would entice parents and other book buyers. Unlike librarians, booksellers were often not knowledgeable about juvenile literature. They knew that bright covers, a "gift" look, or a trendy topic like dinosaurs, attracted customers. And juvenile publishing changed drastically as editors strove to acquire "mainstream" books that would be best-sellers, much as had happened in the world of adult publishing earlier. As one former editor said when asked to define *mainstream:*

> *I'll try not to be too cynical. My understanding of what makes a book "mainstream" is that it has the following attributes: The title and cover illustration clearly convey the content; i.e., you don't have to open the book to know what it's about. It has an easily grasped "handle" or "hook"—bedtime, Halloween, mother love, etc. It is written or illustrated by a famous author or illustrator. It has a strong appeal to adults, either by virtue of its art (nostalgic, "edgy," self-referential, sentimental), or the concept is similar to an already existing successful title. It is inexpensive (except for the "famous illustrator" book, which can be very expensive).*

The first such best-selling commercial juvenile books from trade houses were novelty books like expensive, high-quality pop-ups, which began to appear in the 1970s, and which sold in the tens of thousands. Although libraries bought fewer copies of pop-ups because they were likely to be damaged by their young patrons, bookstore sales more than made up for the lower library sales.

Meanwhile another category—paperback editions of hardcover books—had already made its appearance in the trade and was also helping the bottom line. The main outlet for children's paperbacks was also bookstores, which carried both mass-market and trade editions.

Although there is a difference in trim size and physical quality, the distinction between mass market and trade simply refers to *how* books are distributed. Mass-market channels include newsstands, drugstores, supermarkets, and so on. Mass-market paperbacks are distributed much as magazines are because the first paperbacks in the United States were published and distributed by magazine publishers. Mass-market paperbacks were primarily for adults, though children's paperbacks began to filter in as the demand grew.

Trade paperbacks come directly from trade publishers like HarperCollins, whose Trophy line is printed on good-quality paper instead of high-acid spruce pulp and is a bit more expensive. The mass-market paperbacks from Avon, Bantam, Dell, and Pocket Books are usually sold into stores by one set of publishers' representatives, the trade paperbacks from HarperCollins and other publishers by another. Although the consumer rarely notices the difference, the distinction is important for the writer who wants to understand the market and calculate his estimated income, because the royalty percentages are different.

There is another kind of mass-market book. Sometimes in hardcover, sometimes in paper, the books have low prices and come from Random House, Simon & Schuster, Grosset and Dunlap, and other houses. These books include the original hardcover Nancy Drew and Hardy Boys titles, the Dr. Seuss books, the Little Simon line, the Berenstain Bears, and many other titles. The low prices and bright, commercial art have long caught book buyers' eyes in discount stores, gift shops, some bookstores, shopping mall department stores, and even toy stores.

Other titles are "tie-ins," based on licensed characters from TV shows or movies and can have many incarnations. One set of books featuring a licensed character might be in the supermarket, another in the video store, a different one available only through mail order, yet another one through a book club, and so on. Packagers are usually involved in producing tie-in editions. This is an enormous, if ephemeral, market.

To add to the mix, children are growing up with their own TVs, Walkmans, and computers, and publishers are providing them with multimedia products such as audiotapes and CD-ROMs. As young as its readership, the electronic market was expected to grow fast and wild. Sales of books on CD-ROM have been disappointing, however, and publishers have grown conservative in this area.

It's also still too early to tell how E-books, or books self-published on-line, will fare, but this does not mean that new growth won't occur later on, so writers should be aware of the possibilities of electronic publishing. For the moment, the bookstores are still selling books published in the traditional way, and will be doing so for some time to come.

Added to the commercial and library markets mentioned above is the educational market, which is expanding to keep up with the school population and changes in educational trends. After the optimistic introduction of "whole language" in the 1980s, the pendulum has swung back to "phonics." Tons of textbooks were dumped and other tons bought to take their places. Although sales to schools of trade books have recently declined, Jennifer Brown, children's Forecasts editor of *Publishers Weekly*, noted that sales are still strong because teachers discovered trade books stimulated interest in reading.

To find out more about publishers, you can consult the *Literary Market Place*, which is a weighty annual list of publishers and ancillary enterprises. In addition to names and addresses of publishers (including small presses) in the United States and Canada, the *LMP* contains brief descriptions of publishers and lists the names of editors. One section is devoted to attorneys specializing in intellectual property, another to agents. A separate list is organized by names of people in all these areas, yet another by names of publishers' imprints. The *LMP* also contains a list broken down into categories such as educational and religious publishers. The best place to consult this book is at a library, where it's usually behind the reference desk. Bookstores may also have a copy you can look at, and it's available on-line (at www.bowker.com). Since the *LMP* is so bulky, ephemeral, and expensive, it's not a wise purchase for most writers, but it's invaluable for research.

The most helpful resources for writers of children's books are the Children's Book Council, the Society of Children's Book Writers & Illustrators, the Institute for Children's Literature, and *Publishers Weekly* (see sidebar). Other magazines like *The Writer* and *Writer's Digest* can be useful from time to time since they periodically carry news from the children's book world. The *Children's Book Market,* published annually, is also an excellent reference.

Fortunately, with the advent of Web sites, it's never been easier to do research. However, on-line research is no substitute for going to bookstores and libraries and holding books in your hand. This literal "hands-on" approach, which includes reading the books, is the most satisfying way of getting to know the children's book world.

The marketplace for children's books is like a long corridor. As you walk along it, one door slips shut, another is half-closed or half-open, and another opens wide, welcoming writers. The following chapters will discuss the various markets for manuscripts in greater detail. However, this book is neither the last word nor the most detailed about editors' wants. Since editors leave their jobs and publishing houses move and undergo internal changes, it's important to keep up with the latest news. The sources mentioned in this chapter will endeavor to keep you up-to-date. Nevertheless, before sending in your manuscript, you should telephone the publishing house to be sure the editor you want is still working there and is still accepting unsolicited manuscripts, and to verify the address.

After all, change, like fashion, will not stop. The writer must continue to meet the new challenges of an industry in perpetual transition. However, you may be sure that one thing will remain the same: Writing for children is valuable, enjoyable, and rewarding.

✦ Surfing the Web ✦

For a moderate charge, you can obtain a list of publishers from the **Children's Book Council (CBC)** in New York, or get the list free from its Web site (www.cbcbooks.org). The list, which is frequently updated, contains the names of the major publishers, their editorial and marketing staffs, along with addresses, telephone numbers, and submission policies.

The CBC Web site also provides direct links to most of the member-publishers' Web sites. This is an excellent way to see what is being published at the various houses. The CBC is funded by a group of publishers, and the board of directors consists of editors and other publishing staff. The CBC also maintains a library, open to visitors by appointment, which contains all the books published by the member-publishers during the past three years. The CBC list is indispensable, but note that it does not contain information about every publisher in the United States, only member-publishers.

The Society of Children's Book Writers & Illustrators (SCBWI) offers published and unpublished writers and illustrators memberships in the organization, which has its home office in California; there are also regional divisions and a Web site. Members receive the instructive SCBWI bimonthly newsletter, the *Bulletin,* with articles and current market information. The SCBWI also provides inexpensive lists of magazine, religious, and educational publishers and other materials of value. Joining the SCBWI is highly recommended. Through its regional network you can become acquainted with writers in your area, and other writers are always an excellent source of news. The Web site address, which provides membership information, is www.scbwi.org.

The Institute for Children's Literature in West Redding, Connecticut, is a correspondence school for writers. You do not need to be a student at the school to subscribe to its informative monthly newsletter, the *Children's Writer.* The newsletter is divided into two parts: One carries articles on editors, publishers, trends, and more; the other is the *Marketplace,* which gives specific information on magazine and book markets, including new and small publishers, educational and religious as well as trade. The Web site is www.childrenswriter.com.

To get a quick overview of publishers and forthcoming titles, look into **Publishers Weekly,** a magazine you can find on the Web or at your local library. Twice a year, the spring and fall announcement issues are replete with ads for children's books. A study of the ads and annotated announcements of new books will give you an idea of what publishers are doing *now*. The Web site is www.publishersweekly.com.

6

Quick Like a Bunny

◆

TIPS FOR WRITING PICTURE BOOKS

Happiness makes up in height for what it lacks in length.
—*Robert Frost*

When most people say they want to write a "children's book," they usually mean a "picture book." The picture book is the star of the children's book world. It is a showcase for the illustrator, who may win the coveted Caldecott Medal if her art is spectacular. However, without a text, the artist has nothing to illustrate, so editors are always looking for texts. If you wish to write a picture book, my advice is to do it, but keep in mind that the market is tight; it is harder than ever to place a picture book. You can make it easier if you write one in keeping with the times we live in.

Many adults have no understanding of this genre. They think of children's book writers, illustrators, and editors as milquetoasts who babble on about bunny rabbits. Even worse, so do some neophyte writers and illustrators, who bombard editors with picture books written in sing-song verse about animals with alliterative names like Harry Hare and Bitsy Bunny, poorly illustrated by themselves or an "artist friend." If you have written a book that begins something like, "One day Peter Pigeon (Harriet Hippo, Sally Seal, Walter Wolf) decided to . . ." put it aside and begin work on a new one. Do not use alliterative names. You'll notice that Beatrix Potter used names like Jemima Puddleduck and Jeremy Fisher—names that subtly conveyed the characters' species and even personalities. It was Walt Disney and other cartoonists of the 1930s and 1940s who used alliterative names like Mickey Mouse, Donald Duck, and Bugs Bunny. Although these characters are successful and beloved, they are not book characters but come from comic books and cartoon features and lack the literary stature of such book characters as Kenneth Grahame's Mr. Toad and Lewis Carroll's March Hare. In short, don't be *condescending*. Respect the reader, no matter what age he is.

Most beginning writers think nothing is easier to write than a children's book, and if the result is as follows, they are correct. Consider this typical manuscript:

Imogene Ibex woke up in her bed.
"It's a beautiful day," she said.
Out of her bed she hopped.
Without making a single stop.
Her mom was in the kitchen
But she was itchin'
To go out and play
On such a sunny day.

With art, this text could fill up to three book pages, but so far Imogene hasn't done anything except hop! (Do ibexes hop?) This manuscript is typical of many that come to editors and agents, destined to be returned immediately. It contains predictable flaws such as the forced meter in the lines "without making a single stop" and "to go out and play / on such a sunny day." Words are stuffed into the line simply to fill it up with the right number of syllables. When the writer can't find a rhyme, she comes close, rhyming *stop* with *hopped* and *kitchen* with *itchin'*, which, of course, is cheatin'. As for "her mom," watch out for inappropriate colloquialisms.

Can it be that people who send in manuscripts like this have read no contemporary children's books? Was their most recent encounter with children's verse Clement Clarke Moore's beloved 1823 poem, "A Visit from St. Nicholas"? In meter, rhyme scheme, and strong narrative line ("'Twas the night before Christmas, and all through the house, not a creature was stirring, not even a mouse"), it was in tune with popular culture a hundred years ago.

Of course, not all verse should be damned. Verse in the hands of Mother Goose, Ludwig Bemelmans, or Dr. Seuss can be delightful, and children love rhyme and strong meter, or rhythm, as we know from our own experience. Rhyme and meter are still found in modern songs, especially in the world of rap, which Bill Martin Jr. and John Archambault used to advantage in *Chicka-Chicka Boom-Boom*, illustrated by Lois Ehlert.

Like a poem, a picture book is short, tells a story, and captures an emotional moment. It shows a love of language and has memorable imagery. But it also reflects the literary era in which we live, which is why editors say they don't want to publish books in verse. By *verse*, they mean sing-song verses like those in "A Visit from St. Nicholas," which they regard as old-fashioned.

Some editors have gone so far as to shy away from even the best of verses because they don't trust their own judgment. In short, because of this prejudice, you might as well put away your rhymed story for now. (I have a rollicking one about a frog and cat in *my* drawer.) To be fair, most rhymed stories I've seen have been dreadfully amateurish, which only reinforces the prejudice.

Something comes over people when they sit down to write a children's book, as if they've had a personality change. Many beginning writers think it's de rigueur to tell a story about animals to children. Perhaps their past encounters with children's books surface, and the writing becomes automatic, an echo of some half-formed idea developed in childhood. I'll leave the reason to the psychoanalysts and will confess that my first children's book was based on a newspaper story about a pigeon, which had caught its foot in a clam on the beach.

Beatrix Potter, a sheltered middle-class English gentlewoman, was the mother of today's picture-book animal story. Using animals as stand-ins for people, Potter provided charming, accessible stories to generations of children and their parents. And numerous artists from Don Freeman to Marc Brown have published books with talking animals. Potter was a trailblazer and a genius.

She is, as they say, a hard act to follow. Unfortunately, too many writers saw only that Potter used animals with names and clothing. They failed to see that she was never guilty of being SCAD. The acronym stands for:

1. sentimental
2. condescending
3. anthropomorphic
4. didactic

Memorize these words. They are the cardinal sins of picture-book manuscripts, and they'll be discussed further in this chapter. If your manuscript is guilty of even one of the SCAD sins, your work will likely not even be read to the end. For example, baby talk is condescending and will get a knee-jerk negative response every time.

Nearly all children's picture books deal with homely details, but the very best deal with universal themes as well. Peter Rabbit may have suffered through a life-and-death struggle (universal theme) because he disobeyed his mother (universal theme), but he also had a great time scoffing up the forbidden goodies (universal theme) in Mr. McGregor's garden. Unfortunately, too many writers have imitated the superficial aspects of Potter's work and failed to understand the psychological brilliance underlying it. All her animals are memorable characters, complex in their ways. They are never sentimental, though they are charming, appealing, and lovable. (Note that the best trade editors never use the words *cute* or *adorable* to describe a character.)

The next most important rule in writing for children is that *the protagonist must solve the problem.* Peter Rabbit managed to escape by wriggling under the fence. But in my first picture-book story, a passerby liberated the pigeon's foot from the clam. Although my pigeon, like Peter, had the guts to explore, he did not, like Peter, solve the problem of being trapped. He was a passive hero. As an editor told me, "Thousands of books have been written about individuals wanting to be someone else. Yours has to be different and delightful." It wasn't. It was derivative and dull in spite of its universal theme. Be careful: "Universal" can easily become hackneyed.

Therefore, if you choose to write about animals, imagine that they are people, with quirks and flaws. Choose your animals carefully, matching them to type—without stereotyping or using clichés. Consider all the attributes of a particular animal, not just one. Although technically speaking, your manuscript will be anthropomorphic, if you succeed with your story, it will transcend that classification.

For example, my story would have been different if I had spent some time observing pigeons. I've since learned that a pigeon is patient. It prefers walking to flying. It is always looking for something to eat. It will peck anything on the ground in its search for food. Any one of these characteristics would be enough to inspire a story more original than the one I'd written.

Do they perhaps explain why my pigeon ended up with a clam on its foot? Peck, *slam!*

The writer of the story about Imogene Ibex confessed she didn't know much about ibexes. Since an ibex is so leggy, I have trouble imagining one sleeping in a bed. Still, being leggy, Imogene must be a good runner and kicker, and that's what the writer should have emphasized. I can imagine a book about a chase and a clever use of the art of kicking, not a domestic tale beginning in a kitchen.

Readers can suspend disbelief enough to accept aardvarks, cats, dogs, bears, monkeys, and mice as using their forepaws like hands. An ibex or other large, hoofed animal with "hands" seems too awkward and unnatural to be convincing. Readers will not suspend disbelief, and the editor will decline the manuscript on the ground of anthropomorphism.

What exactly is anthropomorphism? The dictionary says it's endowing animals or machines or even structures with human attributes. When I was a child, *The Little Engine that Could* and *Little Toot the Tugboat* were popular successes featuring "humanized" machines. Today we have the adventures of Budgie the helicopter and the Flying Toaster. (Anthropomorphic? Yes. Best-sellers? Yes. Good books? No. Whoever said children had good taste?)

Even though they are anthropomorphic, animal characters can enjoy adventures denied to children and real animals, and writers and illustrators want to take literary advantage of this freedom. Children can easily cross the invisible line between person and animal or thing. However, if, as a writer or illustrator, you want to cross the barrier between human and nonhuman, you must make the reader suspend disbelief as you would with a fantasy. In general, while stories about talking animals are still being published, stories about talking molecules, buildings, and machinery are not, unless they're written by a celebrity. In other words, sometimes anthropomorphism works, and sometimes it doesn't. Book editors hate cloying anthropomorphism as much as they hate rhyme!

One way to avoid anthropomorphism is to write about children instead of animals. *Blueberries for Sal* by Robert McCloskey is a good example of a realistic picture book that draws a parallel between animal children and human children without being anthropomorphic. Many other writers from Taro Yashima to Tomie de Paola featured children in their stories.

Once you've selected your characters, you must write a story. A series of incidents like the ones in the manuscript about Imogene Ibex is not a story. As Humpty Dumpty told Alice when she was in Wonderland, a story has a beginning, a middle, and an end. (How did Lewis Carroll make us believe an egg could talk?) For example, Peter Rabbit's mother tells him not to go into Mr. McGregor's garden. Peter disobeys. Mr. McGregor chases him and almost nabs him. That is a story. The fact that he and the reader also learn a lesson about the dangers of disobedience is incidental. Heavy-handed stories teaching lessons are *didactic*, and no one likes them, especially children and editors.

If Peter had simply gone for a walk, found Mr. McGregor's garden, and then described everything he saw, we would not be reading about his adventures today. The entry-level reader at the publishing house suspects that's what Imogene Ibex is going to do, and he's already unfolding the self-addressed, stamped envelope the author included. The manuscript will not make it to an editor's desk for a second reading.

Always begin your story in media res—in the middle of the action—instead of with a word like *decided* or with a character's waking up, which only delays the moment of action. Ask yourself where the story begins, and begin it there. For example, "Imogene thought she was alone at the river. Then she saw the lion."

Keep on writing after that. Don't worry about length or anything else until you get to the end of your story. Then ask yourself: Is it a story? What is the conflict? From whose point of view is it told? Are the characters distinct and realistic? Use your word-processing program to count the words. If you have over a thousand, begin to cut out the dead spots. Keep in mind that the future illustrations save you the trouble of describing the characters and setting at length. Delete all unnecessary description.

Once the story satisfies you, cut it apart and tape the sentences in a blank dummy. (You can make a thirty-two-page dummy by folding eight pieces of paper in half.) You are now crafting your story to fit into a format of approximately twenty-six pages, or thirteen double spreads. Most picture books are thirty-two pages long because that is how many pages one large press sheet, known as a signature, can hold. From one to six pages might be front and back matter, which are explained in Chapter 13. See how the story breaks according to the potential illustrations. Are there enough scene changes? Something different and interesting for the illustrator (and reader) must be on each spread. Are the words distributed evenly throughout the dummy, or do some pages run too full and others look too skimpy? Make the appropriate adjustments. Writing a picture book is hard. The writer conveys her ideas in words placed on blank pieces of paper. Not a word, not an action can be superfluous. You must be original, the story must be complete enough to be understood without illustrations, and you must capture the reader's emotions. (If you are an illustrator, you have an advantage, because you can draw what you mean and submit an illustrated dummy.)

If you're a writer and not an artist as well, type your brief text on white bond, double spaced and with paragraphs, and submit it to editors at publishing houses. Do not get an artist friend to illustrate it. Do not illustrate it yourself, not even with stick figures. It has to stand on its own as a story that can be read aloud by a parent, teacher, or librarian. Once you're famous, you'll be able to break these rules, but don't waste your time now.

Many writers have rewritten well-known folk- and fairy tales and had some success. This is not recommended today because editors and illustrators usually do the retelling themselves or hire someone to do it, and most of the popular tales such as "Cinderella" and "Little Red Riding Hood" have been told and retold ad infinitum.

However, with the emphasis on multiculturalism and new immigrant groups in schools, the market for tales from certain cultures—African, Asian, Latin American—expanded, and a demand remains. If you find a remarkable tale that is virtually unknown, it might be worth your while to retell it. Be sure to acknowledge the copyright and find out whether rights are available if you are working from a translation. At Delacorte Press years ago, an illustrator wanted to illustrate a piece by a dead French poet. Jim Bruce, the editor, was enthusiastic. A former professor of French, he helped the artist translate the poem. The artist began his drawings, the book was announced in the catalog—and then it turned out the poet's widow, who was the executor of his estate, refused to grant permission. She didn't think her husband would have wanted the poem published for children! The project was abandoned.

Folk- and fairy tales are a good way for illustrators to break into the picture-book market. Jan Brett retold and accurately illustrated *The Mitten*, a Ukrainian folktale, with great success, and John Scieszka took the folktale format even farther with *The True Story of the Three Little Pigs*. Don't be afraid to be innovative.

If you're an artist who has illustrated either an original story or a folktale, send in a tight dummy and color photocopies of a few pieces of finished art. (Do not send original art until the editor requests it.) A tight dummy is a mock-up of the book with the text pasted in and sketches that are almost finished for each page or spread. Do not do finished art for the entire book. The art director will provide you with specifications after you've signed the contract. Before you can proceed, you'll need to know the trim size, whether the art bleeds or butts, the best media for printing purposes, gutter margin, and many other technical details.

If you've illustrated a friend's story, put the art away for now. Your friend should submit the story on its own, without any art. A neophyte cannot expect to ride into publishing on the coattails of a friend's story. Editors and art directors resent it when authors choose an artist. It remains their prerogative, and, though it is hard to accept, you are hurting your friend's chances if your art is sent in with her story. Editors and art directors review the work of many artists before they select one who meets their needs. They often choose an illustrator whose work is well known and has market value, which is to the writer's (and publisher's) long-term advantage.

If you wish to illustrate children's books, you must make the rounds to art directors with your portfolio or find an artist's agent. Art directors are always interested in seeing illustrations of children and animals in black and white and in color. Your first assignment may well be novels, and a strong black-and-white style will help you get started.

When you write a picture book, try to keep the manuscript to a maximum of four pages, fewer than a thousand words. Long picture books exist, but short ones stand a better chance. The most common criticism you'll hear from the sales reps in publishing houses is "too many words." It's hard to believe that a thirty-two-page book can have too many words, but reps believe consumers want to be able to read the book in a few moments and then buy it on impulse, the way they would a T-shirt.

Once you've written a story that has been accepted for publication, it no longer belongs to you but to the world. The illustrator will open up your story in ways you could never have imagined. Her job is not to reproduce your mind-pictures but to create the world your words evoked for her. The result may delight you or dismay you, but the words are still yours.

Picture books have come a long way since *The Tale of Peter Rabbit* appeared. Writers and artists like Chris van Allsburg, David Macaulay, and David Wiesner have taken the picture book in exciting directions. Before you write or illustrate, go to the bookstore and see what's new.

Having made the journey myself from the pitiful pigeon story to two picture books that were accepted for publication, I have learned that writing a picture book is a joy in itself. Both times the subject moved me, and I therefore lovingly labored to do the best I could with the words. If you don't feel love for the story, put it away. If you do feel the love, you will be compelled to rewrite the story until, as Goldilocks said, it is "just right."

7

How Does the Garden Grow?

◆

WRITING FICTION

There are no shortcuts to any place worth going.
— Beverly Sills

Miss Lillian Davis, the librarian, sat at her big front desk in the center of the Belmar Public Library. No expense had been spared when the one-room library had been built. It stood on a grassy knoll on an acre of land in an affluent residential district in the center of town. Light streamed in through shining Palladian windows.

Timidly, but aware I had the right to do so, I asked Miss Davis for a library card. In turn, she asked me for my name and address. A few moments later, Miss Davis stamped the date on a piece of cardboard and handed it to me. She asked me, "How old are you?"

"Eleven." What a strange question, I thought.

"Go to the left."

I looked wistfully at the loaded bookshelves on the right. "That's the adult section," Miss Davis said. "You can go there when you're in high school."

The idea that children should read certain books at certain ages persists in the juvenile book world. Libraries still have children's departments, though children are no longer drawn and quartered for wandering into the adult section. The "level" issue vexes people not familiar with the children's book market, and if you wish to write for children, you must understand the differences between *age level, grade level, reading level,* and *interest level.* It seems more complicated than it is. (And it's more complicated than it seems.) Librarians and booksellers need to know the age levels or the grade levels of books, because adults will come in and ask for a book "appropriate for an eight-year-old" or "right for a third grader." Therefore, publishers provide age and grade levels in their catalogs and age levels on the books themselves, usually in easily deciphered codes (e.g., 008012) on the jacket flap, sometimes on the copyright page.

Age and grade levels acknowledge that children of the same age may read at different levels of proficiency. Some second graders can read at a fifth-grade level; some fifth graders can read only at a second-grade level—which is why a range is provided.

Editors are the ones who decide what the age and grade levels are, and when the editors were former librarians, they were well equipped to judge. Most other editors guess by the seat of their pants. They feel confident in their choices because they are based on their own reading experience, the difficulty of the texts, and the subject matter. Since age and grade levels usually span three or four years, educated guesses have a good chance of hitting the right number. The difference between a book suitable for ages nine to thirteen and one for ages ten to fourteen is a subtle measure of a speck of maturity. Publishers usually inflate age levels because they believe children will "read up"—that is, read books older than prescribed—but will not "read down"—that is, read books meant for younger children. A number of publishers send manuscripts to reading laboratories to get "scientific" reading levels. Some methods are based on the writer's choices from a list of approved words; others count syllables and words and calculate the ratio. Computer programs also purport to give accurate reading levels.

However, it's not only reading proficiency that determines an age level; interest level is important as well. The only way to be sure of the interest level is to be the person reading the book. When I was ten, I found *Little Women* to be difficult and tedious. At twelve, I thought it the best book I ever read. As an adult, I couldn't finish reading it. The book doesn't change, but the reader does.

Why is it important for the writer to realize that the reading level of a book depends on the reader? As Emerson said, "'Tis the good reader makes a good book." A good reader will struggle through a difficult text. Good readers read books more than once, gleaning something different each time, depending on one's interests at a given moment. The best writers write about what they know and infuse it with their passions. That is the secret of writing for the ages, not magic formulas about age levels.

Therefore, keep in mind that trade publishers' reading levels are only guidelines; they should not be followed slavishly. In 1947, Harper's advertised *Goodnight Moon* by Margaret Wise Brown as suitable for ages three to six. This did not mean that a three-year-old was expected to read it. It meant that the interest level made it suitable to be read *to* a three-year-old. Today, *Goodnight Moon* is read to babies, and children older than six love it too. It brings back pleasant memories of babyhood and validates their sense of having graduated into the "young reader" group. The babies aren't smarter than babies fifty years ago, but the parents are aware that some books can be for children of all ages. Savvy parents also know that children will ask for books to be read over and over, so they are careful to bring home only books that can pass the multiple-reading test—in other words, books they themselves like.

Trade books, including picture books, fit into a long literary tradition. They are supposed to stretch the mind, enrich the reader, inform as well as entertain. They are a counterweight to all the watered-down and overedited texts used in schools. Trade books provide children with the values missing from commercial entertainment such as movies. They also assume children have minds and can use dictionaries. Most novels for teenagers no longer carry age levels, but age levels remain on books for younger readers to guide those who need them, whether parent or bookseller.

Publishers strive to publish books that librarians and booksellers can categorize. On the other hand, some of these categories are becoming extinct or changing, and new ones are appearing. In general, books meant to be read *by* the youngest of children are short, with short sentences and short words. These may be picture books, storybooks, easy readers, or simple books with chapters. One category that almost disappeared is the storybook, which is a long story told in a picture-book format. But the classic storybooks like the Babar books and the Madeline titles are still with us. And not too long ago, readers over seven began to discover the delights of long picture books, such as the Caldecott Medal winner *Snowflake Bentley* by Jacqueline Briggs Martin, illustrated by Mary Azarian.

Like everything else, childhood has been accelerated. Eight-year-olds in jeans, T-shirts, and running shoes don't want to be seen with picture books or storybooks (though they might sneak peeks at them in private). "They're for babies!" they say. They want "real books" with chapters. What they call a chapter book has become a new and thriving genre, broken into categories. In the last two decades, more fiction for first- and second-grade readers has been published than ever before.

Beverly Horowitz is vice president, deputy publisher, and editor in chief at Random House Children's Publishers. Horowitz told me she considers the words *chapter books* to be an educational term, one used in classrooms to indicate that children have reached a certain reading level. It's a child's term, also, she says, a sign that he or she is ready to read a text longer than that in a primer, which may have only one or two words a page.

According to Michelle Poploff, vice president, editorial director of children's paperbacks at Bantam Doubleday Dell (Random House), *chapter book* can also be an "umbrella term." Dell was the original publisher of Patricia Reilly Giff's The Kids of the Polk Street School books, one of the first trade series especially written for second-grade readers. Dell expanded the Yearling line to include chapter books for children between the ages of six and ten. Manuscripts run from about twenty-five to sixty manuscript pages (shorter ones are for younger readers) and usually have black-and-white drawings on most of the pages. As I said earlier about picture books, the protagonists in all juvenile fiction must be active and solve their own problems. Adult characters are welcome, but they must not interfere in the child's story line.

Books for older readers, the "middle-grade," are usually illustrated with six to ten black-and-white drawings and run from 96 to 192 pages. (Teachers sometimes require that students read a book over 100 pages long for a book report. Given the technology of book publishing, many books run only 96 pages—that is, a quantity divisible by 32—so your book may not make it to the book report stage. On the other hand, many children prefer short books.)

When I first entered the children's publishing field, manuscripts for children between the ages of eight and twelve were often declined because they were "episodic"; that is, consisting of loosely connected episodes, each a chapter long, with a minimal plot, about the same characters. In spite of the success of Robert McCloskey's *Homer Price*, few episodic books (although they were not called by that name) were published, with the exception of Joan Aiken's Arabel stories and *Pippi Longstocking* by Astrid Lindgren.

Editors today don't seem to have the same prejudices, and the episodic book has made a comeback. (It was popular in the sixteenth and seventeenth centuries in Europe.) Middle-grade children adore episodic books, because they can read one chapter and put the book down—satisfied—knowing they can pick it up again tomorrow for another story. Sometimes the episodes add up to a plot, and the characters may change and develop over time, but these are not requirements. The stories could continue indefinitely, the way situation comedies do on television. Some contemporary examples of episodic books include *Tales of the Wayside School* by Louis Sachar, *Brooklyn Doesn't Rhyme* by Joan W. Blos, and *The Watsons Go to Birmingham—1963* by Christopher Paul Curtis. These books are just right for children who've graduated from second-grade chapter books but are not ready for older novels. This is also a good place for humorous manuscripts.

The middle-age novel wins the prize, literally, among books for older children: the Newbery Medal. Most of the award-winning books are suitable for ages ten to fourteen. Newbery novels usually address themselves to serious issues such as war, racism, or an individual's struggle for justice. Once a writer has won a Newbery, his or her career is established. Every school and public library will buy a copy, a paperback edition will be issued, and bookstores will carry the book in hardcover at first, in paperback later.

Editors, reviewers, and writers agree that the sine qua non in all literary novels for middle-grade and teen readers is that as the protagonists act in the story, they grow and change.

Also, because of their length, children's novels can usually support only one point of view; that is, the action is seen through the eyes of one character only. The books have coherent plots constructed around a strong conflict, and each action has a purpose.

Here are two examples of writing for different ages. The story is about a brother and sister, Adam and Eve. Note that the reading level is lower for Adam's point of view than for Eve's. His has shorter sentences and words, hers longer, which is natural, because she is older than he is.

Adam dashed into the kitchen. He was in front of his sister, Eve. She tripped over his foot.

"Ouch!" he yelled. He hopped on one foot. He held the toes on the other. He bet they were broken.

"What a dweeb," Eve said. "Wear your shoes. Then your feet won't get hurt."

"Your feet are too big. That's why you trip all the time,"
Adam said. He put his foot on the floor. It hurt. But he could
walk. I'll get even, he thought. He limped out of the kitchen.
"Mommy, Eve broke my foot."

Here's the same incident from Eve's point of view.

"Watch out!" Eve yelled. She tried to catch her balance. Her
dweeby little brother, Adam, had stopped short when they both
ran into the kitchen, and she felt his toes grind under her foot.

She grit her teeth when he yelled, "Ouch!"

"It's your fault," she said. "Mom told you to wear your
shoes."

Adam was hopping around on one foot, cradling the other.
"You broke my toes, you broke my toes," he chanted.

Eve knew he was faking. She probably had hurt him, but he
was making too much of it.

"Mommy," he yelled. "Eve broke my foot." He ran out of
the kitchen.

"I don't need this," Eve said to herself.

Whichever point of view you choose, you can see that the
book immediately sets up certain tensions, such as the sibling relationship and the suspense of discovering how the mother will
handle this situation. The single point of view forces you to focus
on the main character and how he or she acts.

A third benefit is that a single point of view *shows* emotions via crisp dialogue or action rather than through *telling* in artificially long passages of explanatory dialogue. "Telling" how people feel is what leads to condescension and didacticism. Good writing for children encourages them to figure out what is happening, and believe me, they can do so.

Most important, the single child's point of view will relegate adults to the sidelines because the reader will be observing them through a child's eyes. Adults should never—well almost never—be the central characters in a book for children.

However, as I said in chapter 6, *the most important rule of children's books is that the hero has to have a conflict, a problem that he or she solves*. From what we've seen so far, Adam and Eve have no problems except with each other, and those aren't serious; indeed, their rivalry is somewhat trite, but with imagination and skill it can underlie an important plot. Add one or more subplots involving friends, family, or others, and you will add richness to the texture of the novel. The conflict is the source of the plot.

The classic literary conflicts are:

1. hero against another person
2. hero against society
3. hero against nature
4. hero against self.

Literary novels are character driven, not plot driven; therefore, before beginning to write, you must know the main character physically and emotionally. The plot will grow from the character and his personality and how he chooses to deal with the conflict. A useful exercise is to list everything about a character—from what he eats for breakfast to the name of his favorite movie. Name your character; live with him; imagine how he would act in various situations. He is not cardboard; he is a living person.

The most complex characters probably exist in what were once called young adult novels. Librarians, editors, and writers are never satisfied with the definition of a young adult novel, meant for teenage readers. The readers themselves prefer to be called teens, and their books, books for teens. "Young adult novel" used to mean a book written for adults—like *Lord of the Flies* by William Golding or *The Old Man and the Sea* by Ernest Hemingway—that was also suitable for teenagers. It was a book with literary merit, no swear words or explicit scenes involving sexual activity, and on a topic of interest to young people. Life has changed a great deal since that definition held sway. This is one reason librarians cannot agree on an acceptable definition and why novels for twelve- to sixteen-year-olds are often shelved with adult novels.

A teen novel can be one of three types. All should have protagonists who are at least twelve years old. The first type treats subject matter of interest to students in middle school or junior high through high school. A novel, say, about camping—with jokes about falling in the lake and playing tricks on the opposite sex at the next camp—is fine for readers under twelve. At twelve and older, most teenagers would rather read about finding a way to date the kids of the opposite sex at the other camp. Again, it all depends on the age development of the readers. Some are ready for no more than a conversation or maybe a kiss; others may want sexual relations under the stars.

Originally published as young adult novels, some of Paula Danziger's titles, like *The Cat Ate My Gymsuit,* are now considered to be at the low end of the age group. Danziger's books are written simply and appeal to readers from about the fourth grade up. They deal with family problems, social problems, and a touch of romance, only a touch, and are humorous.

The second category would be the novel about teenage concerns like Richard Peck's or P. J. Petersen's books or mysteries like those by Lois Duncan and Joan Lowery Nixon, where the protagonists are teenagers. These books may be found in the junior high libraries because they contain little or no swearing or explicit sex.

The third category might be labeled for "mature" readers and be said to be "edgy." Like Robert Cormier's *Fade* or Francesca Lia Block's *Weetzie Bat,* the books may have street language, sex, or violence treated in a responsible, not exploitative, way. Or the mature teen novel may have little or no sex or violence at all but simply be a thoughtful novel for gifted teenagers and adults, like *Catcher in the Rye* by J. D. Salinger. Considered to be the grandfather of the young adult novel, *Catcher in the Rye* was originally published as an adult book in 1951. We can see how times have changed since then. In the last twenty or thirty years, a number of people who tried to sell books with teenage characters could not find homes for them in the adult divisions of publishing houses. They were happily welcomed by many children's departments.

No matter which of the above genres you choose to write, fiction demands that you know who your characters are, have a general idea of what they are going to do, and how the book will end. You may wonder whether you should outline the plot. For the beginning novelist (and certainly for the writer of nonfiction), an outline is invaluable.

What you need to work on after you have an idea of your plot, theme, and characters is choosing the main action of each chapter. I once began a novel with a long description of the town where the action takes place. Later, this ended up in my reference pile, along with the character questionnaires, not in the book. *Descriptions and explanations are not action.* In other words, some important event must occur in each chapter, so your first step might be to list ten or twelve such events. Also, be sure to set up the time frame: Is the action to take place in one day, one season, one year? Sometimes a chronology or time line helps in mapping out the chapters.

In general, the first four or five chapters serve to introduce the characters and set up the conflicts. By chapter 5, a major event should have taken place. The rest of the book is about resolving the events—with a major turning point coming toward the end—and a satisfactory denouement, tying the loose ends together in a conclusion.

At the same time, each chapter is advancing the plot. Don't play games with the reader. Characters may have secrets from one another, but the reader should be aware of what the protagonist is thinking. You have to plant and foreshadow and establish events throughout, which is easier to do once you're sure of where you're going. You cannot, for example, in the final chapter, say: "He pulled out a treasure map and showed it to his friends. 'Let's dig there,' he said." The reader should have known this map existed from early on and should have had some idea of its contents. You cannot spring a surprise like this on unsuspecting readers at the last minute.

Work in descriptions of people and locations as you go along, and sprinkle in subtle clues to the characters' personalities. Dig into your reference pile to make sure that your geography is consistent, your characters' names are the same—in other words, Eve stays Eve and does not become Eva. Consider the themes of the book, and create events to highlight them.

A common problem with many first novels is poor staging. The characters seem to be floating in outer space, not set firmly in a definable area such as a kitchen, garden, football field, and so on. The writer must help the reader see what the writer is seeing in her mind's eye. You don't need much, a detail or two will suffice, as in this passage:

They went through the gate of the cemetery, up a path beneath
trees centuries old. Eve's feet crunched the fallen leaves on the
path. From time to time she glanced at the tombstones and
monuments as she passed them by.
  "What's that?" Adam cried.

And then there's the opposite flaw. Cataloging each trivial movement, each item, obsessively. Learn how to condense the information and provide only the essentials. Do not write, for example:

Eve looked at Adam. He was standing ten feet away from her on
the path. He was pointing at something. She couldn't see what it
was. She walked up to him. As she walked, she read the names
on the tombstones aloud to give herself courage.
  "Abbott, Nestor, Baciagalupo, Partridge . . ."

This is not the time for Eve to drag her feet. "Eve ran up to Adam and looked where he was pointing" will do the job.

Unfortunately, until the writer of serious novels for young people wins the Newbery, his career may languish in the shadows of the land called Midlist, novels by writers who are not well known or who have not had a "blockbuster" best-seller. Bookstores still carry almost no juvenile fiction in hardcover because it does not sell well enough. The few you see will be prizewinners or by popular authors. Libraries with reduced budgets may not be able to afford novels by little-known writers. It used to be that when a midlist book went into paperback, the writer could hope for decent sales, but that's no longer true, for reasons to be discussed later. Nonetheless, it's important to persevere in spite of the obstacles, because the road to fame still begins with the midlist, novels by writers yet to be discovered.

Hone your writing skills. Chapter 9 contains more writing tips and will help you edit your work. It remains true that the more you write, the better you get, and the more you *can* write. The field is always wide-open for books that are funny or serious, timely or historical. One bookseller recently lamented the lack of books about prehistory! Will she be heard in New York? Will prehistory be the next trend? Who can tell? Don't worry about trends. Write your book and worry about publishing it later.

A few years ago, I traveled to Chincoteague in Virginia to see the annual pony swim described in Marguerite Henry's classic, *Misty of Chincoteague*. I felt as if I were on a pilgrimage. While there, I bought and reread the book, which was on sale in one of the few souvenir stores. In the newspaper, I read about Misty's great-granddaughter, who had just foaled at the age of twenty-three. People lined up after the pony swim to watch the movie, presented at no charge in the local theater. About seventy thousand other people—mostly families with "middle-aged" children—attended the pony swim, an event that has changed little since 1947, when the book was published. The pony swim is not a "media event," and Chincoteague is not a garish theme park out to gouge the tourist; it is a community with pride in its heritage.

This experience validated my own feelings about the beauty and value of the best children's books. I know that somewhere in a library a child is running her fingers along the spines, looking for a book to read. Maybe she'll find yours, and maybe the delight of reading it will remain in her memory for a lifetime.

8

Bunnies in the Money

◆

SHOULD YOU WRITE A SERIES?

Miracles happen to those who believe in them.
—Bernard Berenson

Almost every writer has dreamed of creating a successful paperback series. Notable best-selling series like Choose Your Own Adventure and the Baby-Sitters Club were published in the 1980s, and by the 1990s, others, like Goosebumps and the Animorphs books, became blockbuster properties. Publishers were crying out for more, and writers were eager to gain fame and fortune this way. It turned out to be easier to marry royalty.

First, all the successful series above have an easily grasped hook or identity. Second, a series has to be on a topic that appeals to children or teenagers. Third, it has to be fresh and unique. Writers and editors have been racking their brains for years to come up with concepts for series. The same ideas have been batted back and forth across conference tables at paperback publishing houses as well as among writers. Mention a topic, any topic—it's been done or thought of. Yet you and I know that come next season, some series will hit the charts with an idea so simple that we will berate ourselves for not having thought of it ourselves.

If there are no new ideas, there are new ways of executing them, and the challenge for the writer is to find that new way, a way that is in tune with the third millennium. As Jean Feiwel, publisher and editor in chief at Scholastic, told me, "Tried-and-true themes to which an author has given her own spin can be highly successful, but she better be current in her language and details." The best place to look for those themes, language, and details is at home or wherever there are children. If I were to tell you what's hot with kids right now, it would be out-of-date before this book could get published. During a visit in 1998 to an elementary school, I mentioned that I'd been to the former Soviet Union. The children asked me, "When?" I answered, "1990." They began to laugh. "What's so funny?" One child answered, "That's when we were born." Lordy, lordy, it's bad enough to reach forty, but to be passé after such a short time in an adult life is sobering, indeed.

So forget about what worked in 1985 or even 1995. As Feiwel also said: "Do not follow what is being published with your own version of the concept. It's been done, and we don't need another one. We need something different." Think about 2005 or even later, then write down the concept and series title. After that, she suggests, prepare a series proposal, two or three pages long, in which you name and describe the characters and give plot summaries for *twelve* books. As Feiwel said: "The idea must have the potential for continuity, for many different kinds of stories featuring the same characters and concepts. This was true of the Baby-Sitters Club, but we learned to our regret that it was not true for the Sleepover Club—how many sleepovers can you have?"

If you are a successful writer with a track record, you can probably get away with writing and submitting a few chapters of the first book in the series. If you are an unknown, you should write a complete book. However, contrary to what you might expect, my advice is that an unknown writer should send in the complete book only, not the series proposal. If an editor expresses interest in the book and makes an offer, *then* tell her you want to write a sequel or a series.

Here are two examples of how two different writers managed to create series. One is by a writer with several published books behind her, Gibbs Davis, and one by a former neophyte, Betsy Duffey. Davis is the author of the series White House Ghosthunters. This is what she told me about how the series evolved:

I had recently visited the White House and learned that over two hundred kids had once lived there. Sparking my imagination with the old "what if" exercise so useful to writers, I imagined, What if the daughter of the president of the United States were a budding detective and solved mysteries in the famous house?

I drew up a proposal and wrote some sample chapters, and my agent sent the material out. Eventually, Jill Parsons at Pocket Books offered a contract.

Soon after, over lunch with Jill, she told me how much she liked my proposal, but, she said, the concept needed to be stronger. That's when I mentioned that during my research I had discovered the White House was the most haunted house in the country. Jill's eyes lit up as she took the concept one step farther. "What if the ghosts of past presidents and first ladies secretly help our young sleuth?" We looked at each other and knew that was it!

I then took the important step of testing the new concept with children and adults with this sentence: "The daughter of the president of the United States (her mother) solves mysteries in the White House with help from the ghosts of past presidents and first ladies." The children responded to the fantasy of living in the White House, while adults loved the entertaining blend of mystery and history.

Every series has to have appealing characters, but it's vital to find a concept that has legs, that can go the distance from book to book. I knew White House Ghosthunters would provide an unending supply of interesting characters and dramatic situations.

The evolution of Betsy Duffey's series about George and his dog, Lucky, took a different course. *A Boy in the Doghouse* was first published in hardcover at Simon & Schuster, illustrated by Leslie

Morrill. As the editor, I felt that Duffey's title had two words in it, *boy* and *dog*[house], with an immediate appeal to readers, so perennially popular it's hard to write about them without being trite. However, *doghouse* indicated amusing troubles—and that was also appealing. The book was exceptionally well written, it had a funny twist, and it was informative on the subject of training a puppy. It had the spark. It couldn't miss, and it didn't. Reviews were excellent, and so were sales in both hardcover and paperback. The success of *A Boy in the Doghouse* led to Duffey's being asked to write more books and to create a series, with each book having the dog's name, Lucky, in the title. Again, stories about a boy and his dog are infinite. Duffy has since gone on to create several other successful series.

As a new agent, I took on a few writers who presented complete proposals and finished novels to kick off a series, which I sent around to various publishers; I was unable to sell their work, even though the editor in me thought the concepts were strong. One was a girls' sports series; the other was about a rock band in a New York City high school. Editors said things like "We already have books about girls and sports on our list," and "Books set in New York don't sell." To be honest, the novels were not well written and needed a great deal of editorial work. I'd had the mistaken notion that editors would be willing to work with these writers if they felt the concepts were strong. I'm quite sure the weak writing was at least half the cause of the books' being declined.

Because of these and other experiences, I would encourage beginning writers to build up a track record by writing one good book at a time, as Duffey did. If the book takes off, your editor may ask you to do either a companion novel (literary jargon for a sequel) or a series.

Once you are, like Davis, known to librarians, reviewers, and readers—and have an agent—selling a series will be a little easier. Writers may be surprised at how modest an advance may be for a new series. Publisher and writer both are investing in the future success of the books, and publishers are cautious. Your editor and publisher are taking a chance on something new because they have had time to get to know you and your capabilities.

Sometimes it seems that anyone can predict which book will be a best-seller, that it's like a disease, presenting signs that would cause it to erupt. I was incredulous when I overheard Peter Ritner, editor in chief of adult trade at Macmillan in the 1960s, say, "No one can tell which book will be a best-seller." I've learned he was right.

No matter how clever and timely your idea may be, the chances are that you will not be the only one writing on that subject—and many others that simultaneously reach the attention of writers. The trick is to put your own imagination to work on the idea. New twists on ideas are always welcome. We live together in the same society and are exposed to many of the same influences. Therefore, coincidences happen. A successful TV series for adults might inspire a writer to undertake a juvenile version. Every two years we watch the Olympics on TV. Naturally, that's a series topic many writers consider. Another way to write a book the stores will want is to write something trendy, but timing is everything. You almost have to be able to foretell the future and know what will be all the rage two or three years before it happens.

Let's say you decide to develop a series called Gopher Broke. You write one book and a proposal, send it out, and you find an editor who adores it! Once it's clear that gophers are hot, every paperback house will be sure to want gopher books, but it'll be too late, because your gopher books were out there first and are selling like hot dogs at Coney Island. By the time the imitators get into the stores, the craze may be over. If the genre is strong enough, as with horror or mysteries, one or two imitators may survive as well. This can happen. It has happened!

People have also won the lottery. Sure, it's fun to think up concepts and catchy titles, but it's also hard work and extremely speculative to develop the books themselves. If truth were told, series publishing is part inspiration, part guesswork, part talent, great marketing, and tons of luck.

Although editors will deny it, series ideas have been stolen, which is another reason not to offer series proposals indiscriminately. One young writer told me she'd written a series with characters that had unusual names. It was turned down by a publisher, but shortly thereafter, the same publisher launched a series with only a slightly different concept. One of the books had a character with the same name doing the same thing as in her series. Was the idea stolen? I have no idea. I prefer to think an editor subconsciously absorbed the idea and then suggested it to another writer. As for the characters' having the same unusual name, that could have been a coincidence.

In another case, a young writer had an idea for a series, and the publisher was gung ho. A contract was almost in the offing, when the editor decided to decline the series. A season or two later, a famous writer came out with the same series idea from the same publisher. The young writer cried, "Foul!" but the affair was hushed up; even the writer's agent told him to forget what had happened.

A number of cases such as this have occurred in the adult world and have drawn attention from the media. Some writers have won their cases; others have not. A young adult book I edited by a well-known juvenile and adult writer became a blockbuster movie for all ages with no acknowledgment of the original source. The writer was told he couldn't prove his book had inspired the movie, and the case never even made it to court.

Old codes of ethics and honor have disappeared as some aggressive and eager editors take on the habits of Hollywood and network TV. If you value your idea, keep it to yourself and a few trusted friends. If your idea pops up in an article or review in *Publishers Weekly* before you've even begun your book, you'll know that it was the result of a coincidence, not loose lips.

Although they are of a different nature, nonfiction series are popular with some trade publishers and educational publishers whose work is aimed mainly at the school library market. One way to learn about these publishers is to peruse their catalogs. If a series on a particular topic has many different authors, you can write to the editor and suggest doing a new book; some series are open-ended. Or you might suggest an entire new series on your own. Publishers find it easier to market series, a group of related books, to the library market. So think big. Again, be warned that all the good ideas have been taken—except for the new one from you. Publishers already have series on countries, social problems, women's biographies, science, math, history; whatever is taught in schools or featured in the news.

The good news about nonfiction series is that often the writer need not write the whole book before receiving a contract. An outline, three complete chapters, and perhaps a statement about why a book on this topic is needed will suffice. If you are writing about the life of girls in ancient Egypt and you know ancient Egypt is studied in third grade, be sure to mention this. It will help the editor position the book. Three chapters are enough to tell the editor whether you can write. She may trust you to finish the rest according to your outline. Nonfiction writers are usually asked to supply the illustrations for the book. It would be premature for you to submit actual photos and artwork, but you should consider the value of presenting photocopies of the art you will furnish from photographic sources.

If you prefer to try a single title, you can send it to some of the trade publishers who do nonfiction. Some nonfiction writers worth emulating are Penny Colman, Russell Freedman, and James Giblin. All three write well and do impeccable research on a variety of topics from women doing defense work in World War II to Abraham Lincoln to chimney sweeps, subjects they clearly love.

These writers—and others—have written many award-winning nonfiction books that appeal to young people and sell well in bookstores and to libraries.

It's always a good idea to talk to teachers and school librarians about which subjects are studied in different grades and what may be needed to help fill out a reading list. Some subjects, like health and social studies, are studied in nearly every grade, but the level of information varies according to age. The youngest children are introduced to the idea that tobacco is a drug, for example, but older children learn more about other drugs and their effects.

You may also be able to find freelance writing work on a series with a packager, or book producer. Both trade and educational publishers buy books that packagers have developed. Packagers have long existed to create books for publishers, but the 1970s and 1980s saw many new companies such as Cloverdale Press, Dan Weiss Associates, Mega-Books, and Parachute Press come into existence.

Not only do packagers create series, they work on material commissioned by the owners of licensed material. Have you noticed the increase in TV programs for young people, especially (though not exclusively) on Nickelodeon, the Disney Channel, and PBS? Many writers are supporting themselves by writing tie-ins on a work-for-hire or royalty basis for book packagers and publishers. TV series have spawned quite a few lines of books, with *Sesame Street* and *Barney* heading the list for the toddler set. Other TV and book series, like *Wishbone* and *Malcolm in the Middle,* are being directed to older viewers and readers. Pokemon is probably the first computer game to become a hot series of books. But what's hot today will be cold by the time you read this book. The mass-media world moves fast.

Movie studios like Disney and DreamWorks each produce at least one major movie a year, which gets the full tie-in licensing treatment, from toys at Burger King to bed linens and books. The largesse from a major motion picture is spread around to many different suppliers and vendors.

How is such a massive effort coordinated? It begins two to three years before the release date of the movie, when the studio has already prepared a set of guidelines for distribution to interested parties. The guidelines contain artwork and strict rules on how to present the various characters so that they look alike no matter who produces the final product. The book rights are often shared among the different publishers, who bid on them. Random House may buy the mass-market hardcover picture-book rights, Avon the paperback tie-in license, Grolier a mail-order book-club deal. No matter how the tie-in market works, writers are wanted, but it's not always clear who the publishers and packagers of the various titles are.

How do you find out? If you live at the End of the World and have no access to any of the publications mentioned in chapter 5, you can write to the publishers of the series books. The publisher's name and address are always on the copyright page. If you see a line like "Produced by Felix Press, Inc.," it means Felix Press (not a real firm) was the book producer. You can find that address either through the American Book Producers Association in

New York City, the SCBWI *Guide to Book Packagers/Producers*, or in *Literary Market Place*. You could also try the national telephone directory assistance services, which may be able to help. If none of these gets results, write to Felix Press in care of the juvenile editorial department at the publisher and ask that your letter be forwarded.

If you consult the SCBWI *Bulletin* or the *Children's Writer* regularly, you'll have an edge. These publications provide information on who is looking for what and where they are located. Because they always need dependable writers, many packagers look at unsolicited material. It's also not a bad idea to read the entertainment trade publications like *Variety* to find out about possible assignments based on a future film or TV project. For the writer, by the time something is featured in a *consumer* publication like *People*, it's too late. The best way to find out about freelance projects is to join a writers' group and network with other writers and the editors, many of them freelance, who work for packagers.

Writing on demand can pay well, with advances ranging from about $1,000 to $10,000 per book, depending on the series. Usually the work is done for a flat fee or on a "for hire" basis, and no royalty is paid. Your byline may or may not be used. (The Nancy Drew series, for example, has the pen name Carolyn Keene on all the titles.) Finally, the writer must relinquish all rights to his written material and may be asked to sign a document promising to keep all the information he's been given confidential.

Writing series books based on licensed characters is different from writing trade books. Series editors are pressed for deadlines and rarely have time to praise the writers, who must adhere to the writing criteria of the series. Perhaps the hardest part is the time constraint. More than once, the writer may have submitted the manuscript in time, but the publisher hadn't read it for months—and then asked the writer for a complete revision a week before the manuscript was due to the printer. The book has been announced; it must be published on time. Without your permission, sections are slashed or rewritten; the book may even be given to another writer for a rewrite. Writers must be extraordinarily resilient and professional to withstand such treatment.

On the other hand, the writer may take great pleasure in telling her family and friends that she wrote a book based on a TV show everyone has heard of, and that it's available in nearly all bookstores. Her prestige will shoot up among the people who never paid attention to her literary work. The writer will also have learned a great deal about her craft from her demanding editor. Writing a mass-market paperback series for a packager can be an excellent way to become a better writer. And it may be a way for a writer to develop the network and track record she needs to propose a series idea of her own.

Here is a heartening story to keep in mind, about a writer who had written a number of series for various publishers, with none being a success. She then proposed a new series to Scholastic. Feiwel, who asks only that she be given "something I haven't seen before," was enthusiastic. But though she and her staff at Scholastic had faith in the idea, they suggested a change in the name. They then coordinated all the elements necessary to promote a series, creating a package that had good timing, sequence of titles, and publicity. At first booksellers were reluctant to take on the series, because the author did not have a stellar track record. Scholastic insisted. The rest is history, as they say. Katherine Applegate's series, originally called Changelings, became a hit called Animorphs. The trail of unsuccessful series gave Applegate the writing experience to follow through with her successful one. As the Ukrainian proverb has it, "Winter snow brings spring flowers."

9

Inside the Fence

✦

To see what is in front of one's nose requires a constant struggle. —George Orwell

By now Gus had come to understand how the publishing field has changed in recent years. He'd also written a novel and wanted to send out the manuscript right away.

"Hold on," I told him. "Submitting your book hot off the computer is a mistake."

"But I finished it. I want to get it out of the house. I know an editor will buy it as soon as she reads it."

"Right," I answered, fingers crossed.

Writers will improve their chances if they wait a day or even a week or more until their excitement abates, allowing passions to cool. Go over your manuscript with an objective eye, a pencil in your hand. A manuscript with too many errors will annoy editors and make them doubt your abilities. And it wouldn't hurt, since we all have blind spots, to ask a friend to mark misspellings, typo-graphical errors, and faulty punctuation. Even a computer spelling program cannot distinguish between *its* and *it's*.

In the following excerpt from "An Owed to the Spelling Checker," circulated on the Internet, Dave Burnham wrote:

I have a spelling checker.
It came with my PC.
It plane lee marks four my revue
Miss steaks aye can knot sea.

Eye ran this poem threw it,
Your sure reel glad two no.
Its vary polished in it's weigh,
My checker tolled me sew.

It's also a good idea for writers to read their texts aloud, es-pecially picture books. Since parents, teachers, librarians, and other adults read books aloud to children, the way the text sounds is important. Reading to children is also a good idea; they are honest critics. You'll quickly learn from them where the manuscript falters and dead spots lurk in your text, as well as what makes the audience laugh or sigh. Many writers submit manuscripts saying they've tried it out on children, who adored it. However, *never, ever, tell this to an editor!* It's quite possible that the child simply enjoyed sitting in your lap and would have tolerated a software manual. Children can have the worst taste in the world, and, as Dr. Seuss discovered, you can make them laugh with the most obvious of jokes, such as funny-sounding names. Laughter is infectious, and once one child in a group begins to giggle, the rest will too. They also tend to fidget during the serious parts. Take this as a sign that your text may be too wordy or over their heads, and revise accordingly.

Zena Sutherland, the noted literary critic, once scolded the committee members discussing potential award-winning books at a meeting of the American Library Association and forbade them to say "I liked it" or "I didn't like it." She was right to do so. Like or dislike is not the issue. Literary criticism includes evaluating books with an eye to effective characterization, plausibility, universality of theme, motivation. Also, different people, including children, have different tastes, and a book that bores one child may delight another.

The editorial problems listed here are by no means complete, but this is a good place to begin your own critique of your manuscript.

1. *Effective writing depends on showing through action, dialogue, or detail.* Don't think that children need everything spelled out, because it leaves little for the reader to imagine. For example, picture two children alone in a graveyard at night.

> *"Did you hear something?" asked Adam.*
> *"No," said Eve. She stumbled.*
> *"What's that?" Adam asked.*
> *"Only an open grave."*

What should you write next? Should you say, "Adam was frightened"? Or have him say, "I want to go home"? The first is telling, the second is showing. (It's also clear from these four sentences that Eve is in charge and unafraid.)

Let the showing do the work; don't tell the reader what to think or feel. If you wrote your manuscript on a word processor, use the Find command to search for every use of *felt*. Then examine each sentence: Are you telling instead of showing? You may have more work to do, after all.

2. *Does each scene and incident in the book advance the plot or develop the characterization?* Are you certain you're not just filling up space on the page, because you didn't know what else to say? Be sure you're not going off on tangents enthralling to you but meaningless to your reader, who would rather you dealt with your characters and plot. In the heat of composition, everything seems relevant to the book, and the temptation to throw it all in is great, especially for writers using word processors. Hard-hearted as you may be, it's a rare writer who cuts all the beloved irrelevancies and tangents; a good editor might do the rest, provided you've not so bored her that she refuses to finish reading your book.

3. *None of the characters in your book should be perfect*, that is, as one-dimensional as Nancy Drew, who *is* perfect. In formula fiction (which many paperback series are), characters are fantasies, because that's what the readers want: a princess, a prince, and a rival, or a good twin and an evil twin, or space explorers who never

get killed. But literature shows that people are complex, with plots growing out of their faults as well as their virtues. Take a hard look at each of your characters. Each one should have good traits and flaws. The more human your characters, the more memorable they'll be. Take an especially hard look at old people, small children, and villains. They are the easiest to stereotype, to the point where they become ludicrous caricatures.

✦ Character Description ✦

This is a useful exercise to help you define your characters, especially the main ones. Just for fun, imagine your protagonist is Peter Rabbit as you read the exercise.

- What is his (her, understood) name? Sex? Age?
- Where does he live?
- Are his parents married or single or widowed or divorced?
- Does he have siblings and other important relatives?
- Who arc his friends?
- Who are the people he dislikes or who dislike him?
- What is his personal life like? Hobbies, interests, pets?
- What is his favorite color?
- What does he eat for breakfast? Who prepares it?
- What does he want?
- What is the conflict or obstacle to getting it?
- Where is the suspense in the plot?

> When you use the exercise for your characters, you may
> not be able to fill in the blanks immediately, but as you write,
> the other information will come forth from your unconscious.

4. Dialogue shows character, and *each character should sound like himself*, but be on the alert for the kinds of caricatures you still see on TV. Few grandmothers today wear iron gray hair in a bun, granny glasses, and long aprons and use phrases like "Land's sake, young man. You are a caution." Grandmothers, mothers, aunts, teachers, and librarians use contemporary expressions, and many wear jeans and T-shirts.

The following passage from Todd Strasser's novel, *How I Changed My Life*, demonstrates how he handled dialogue by different persons. These are the reactions from strangers in a pizza parlor to Bo's new hairdo when her friend Bobby asks:

> *"Doesn't she look great? . . . Would you believe she's terrified that the kids at school are going to laugh at her?"*
>
> *"No way. She looks gorgeous," said one of the countermen.*
>
> *"What do you care what other people think?" asked one of the big-hair girls.*
>
> *"They're just jealous, honey," said one of the overweight grandmothers. . . .*
>
> *"If anyone laughs at you, smash 'em in the face," said one of the twelve-year-old Marlboro smokers.*

It's only fair to mention that Strasser spent several years writing for TV, where he learned how to refine the writing of dialogue. If editors say you have trouble with dialogue, consider taking a playwriting course and keep your ears open to how the people around you speak. Note the use here of *overweight* instead of *fat*. Bo, the narrator, is being euphemistic, and there's more about euphemism later in this chapter.

5. *Avoid long descriptions of people and places.* Many writers get carried away and describe everything a character is wearing. Sometimes this is done to fill up the pages. Other times, writers think it's necessary for the reader to know exactly what everyone looks like. Again, trust the reader to fill in the blanks, and cut back on the adjectives. When a telemarketer calls you, don't you immediately imagine from the voice alone what he or she looks like? I do that as soon as a character speaks in a book. Note how succinctly Strasser describes his characters above.

Appearance should be mentioned briefly and only if it matters; that is, if it's a clue to character or has some other function in the story, such as showing how the character plans to impress someone of the opposite sex.

> *Eve couldn't decide how to do her nails. Blue to show she was with it? Red to show she was sexy? Green to show she was daring? She studied her hands. No matter how she tried, she couldn't help biting her nails to the quick. She reached for the bottle of clear polish. Would it look strange if she wore white gloves all night? she wondered. Maybe she'd start a trend.*

Whatever you do, please don't have the character look in the mirror so that we can find out what she looks like. This worked in *Snow White and the Seven Dwarfs*, but that was in 1815.

Similarly, do not describe the landscape or the interiors of rooms in fine detail. Set the scene as briefly as you can without neglecting "the details that give a book its richness," according to Joan Aiken. Use details that count, adding color, texture, life— and, above all, meaning. Evoke the atmosphere of a room with a few phrases such as "velvet curtains" or "shoes piled on every surface." For example, in *The Pawloined Paper*, when I wanted to *show* how vain yet insecure a villain was, I decorated his room with portraits of himself.

6. *"Omit needless words,"* advised William Strunk in 1935. This is still excellent advice. One of the first things to look for is *periphrasis*, taking the long way to say something. For example, some writers still worry about repeating nouns, including proper nouns, and will try to use other words in their place. Help your readers keep the characters straight by using their names or a pronoun instead of descriptions.

> *"I want to go home," Adam said.*
> *"Don't be silly," Eve said. "It's just a hole in the ground."*
> *The boy began to cry.*

Boy? What boy? Oh, Adam. *That* boy. . . . Two words instead of one.

It also drives me crazy when a writer keeps reminding me of a person's job, even though we know his name.

Eve's mother's friend, Bob, was a waiter at the Pizza Grill, where they were eating. "Hi," said Bob when he came over to their table. He was handsome, Eve thought while he was being introduced to them. The waiter took their orders and went to the kitchen.

The waiter? Right, Bob.

It's so easy to write, "There is . . . ," but be warned and avoid those two words, especially in fiction. Highlight "there is" (and "there are," "there was," "there were") whenever they appear, and rephrase the statement if you can. The usage is correct, but the effect is dullness. With all its faults, advertising has perfected vivid, active writing, and I can't recall any ad that used a variation of "there is."

Also insidious is the creep of verbal clutter like extra wire coat hangers. In a mistaken attempt at emphasis, the following words automatically flow out of our fingers as we write: *just, really, very, all,* and *now.* Erase them. Put back only the ones you really need—I mean, you need. See?

Suddenly, quickly, and other such adverbs, especially at the beginning of a sentence, fail to convey speed because they slow down the reader, interfering with his getting to the all important verb. ("Suddenly, she fell into the open grave.") It seems that a transitional adverb is required, but that's because the sentence is not strong enough. Consider: "Eve stumbled. 'Yeow!' she screamed. She fell into the open grave." (Whoops! Delete *open*; not required because self-evident).

It's not nice to hate, but the word *somehow* makes me see red. What does it mean? If it means you have no idea ("Somehow I'll get even"), it's all right. But if you do know either intuitively or because you have good reasons for knowing, let the reader in on the secret. Don't write, "Somehow, Eve got out of the grave"; tell us how she did it. Watch out, too, for *something*, and *thing*, which are also vague. If the right word doesn't come to mind while you're writing, put in a vague one, but find a substitute when you revise!

Steer clear, too, of meaningless vogue words like *incredible*, *amazing, awesome, tremendous*, which, like *colossal, awful, gigantic*, and *huge*, have lost their force through being overused. Save powerful words for the right occasion, such as a volcanic explosion or the birth of octuplets.

7. *Learn the verbs of speech*. Nothing looks so amateurish as the sort of dialogue attribution found in many mass-market books. People sigh, joke, and lie, smile, remind, and breathe sentences. These are not legitimate verbs of speech. Do not write: "'Your nails look great,' she smiled." It should be: "'Your nails look great.' She smiled." (If you find yourself using *smiled* often, you are relying on it to convey emotion. Go back and work on your dialogue. The same is true for *nodded*.)

Whispered, mumbled, and *bellowed* are verbs of speech, but they should be used sparingly, only when the occasion demands it. One of the worst offenders is *hissed*—which is a verb of speech but should not be used when there are no *s*'s in the sentence!

Effective dialogue does not require adverbs after the verbs of speech because the dialogue conveys the emotion. Writers of mass-market romances and series are usually telling their readers what to think, so they tack adverbs on after illegitimate verbs of speech like this: "'I'll never see him again,' she sighed longingly." To be honest, many mainstream writers get away with prose like this in the hardcover market, too.

The current trend is to keep attribution simple, using words like *said* and *answered* but not *replied*, because it is too formal and sounds dated. Write dialogue so that the reader knows who is speaking without your having to attribute the words. This works best, of course, when only two people are speaking.

You can also avoid direct attribution by having the character act and speak in the same passage, as in "Goldilocks sat down. 'This chair is too high.' She got up and sat in Mama Bear's chair."

8. *Avoid the passive voice* whenever possible. Although it's correct, the passive voice results in flat writing because it's impossible to see an invisible agent, which is why it's so often used—or, to use the active voice, why bureaucrats use it so often. A simple example: "Make sure your name is spelled correctly." If it isn't, no one is responsible, because we don't know who did it! (That's the government for you!) In the following example, which sentence is more vivid: "The land was settled by farmers" or "Farmers moved in and settled on the land"?

9. *Does your book have a voice?* As an editor and agent, I've seen many unsolicited manuscripts that fell into what I called a gray middle, like overcooked vegetables without salt. The characters and plot were promising, but the writing style was undistinguished. All the words were in the correct places, but the manuscript lacked a voice, a style.

In books for young adults, the voice is often that of the narrator. Richard Peck has said his first-person narrators always sound older and more intelligent than the intended readers. The reader thinks she's older and wiser than she is, and doesn't want to read a story told by someone who's still wet behind the ears. Peck strikes the balance between contemporaneity versus formality with consummate skill and thought.

You are who you sound like, as George Bernard Shaw demonstrated in *Pygmalion*. Take a look at the early work of the greatest writers: It, too, lacked style. Your voice will arrive after experience and practice, just as it did when you discovered your own style of dressing.

10. *Collect and savor verbs.* Good writers love verbs the way good cooks love herbs. Flat writing is the result of using tired verbs, along with all the faults listed above. To avoid monotony, to convey different kinds of action, to move your work along, you need verbs, especially for simple, everyday actions. You should own a copy of *Webster's New Dictionary of Synonyms*, which, unlike a thesaurus, gives the sources of usages and discriminates among synonyms. Each page is a revelation.

Also, use verbs, not participles, when trying to convey separate, *consecutive* actions. For example, "Adam ran to the edge of the grave, lay down on the grass, and stared at Eve" is better than "Running to the edge of the grave, Adam lay down on the grass and stared at Eve." (He can't run, lie down, and stare at the same time, but lazy writers defy logic.) Participles should be used only with *simultaneous* actions: "Looking up at Adam, Eve shouted, 'Get me out of here!'"

11. *Pay attention to the little words like prepositions*, the correct use of which can be one of the most vexing points in English usage. The writer should know when to use *in* and when *into*, when *on to* and when *onto*. He does not have his characters "enter into" a room or go "outside of" the house, because *into* and *of* are redundant. Words like *incorporate* and *exit* carry the preposition within, the joey in a kangaroo's pouch, as it were, so there's no need to "incorporate into" or "exit out of." You do need the *of*, however, after *couple*, as in "a couple of grapes." In New York City, people stand "on line," but elsewhere, they stand "in line" and go "on-line" when they use the Internet. Observing the fine distinctions, such as using "compare with" instead of "compare to" will strengthen your command of the craft of writing.

Because of space constraints, journalism has done its share to cause language to become sloppy. As it becomes more clipped, so does thought.

12. *Watch your usage.* Pernicious influences attack the English language from all sides: advertising, business, street slang, pretentiousness. In the 1950s, when Winston cigarettes were advertised as "tasting good, like a cigarette should," thoughtful people were

more dismayed at the flagrant bad grammar than at tobacco.

Soon thereafter the third edition of the Merriam-Webster unabridged dictionary was published, causing even more alarm. The editors of this influential dictionary produced the first waves on the shore of permissiveness, or loosening of standards, which came to characterize the last part of the twentieth century. Unlike its predecessor, the still revered second edition, the third edition did not *prescribe*, or differentiate between what was "the preferred usage among educated people," but *described*, that is, recorded "common usage." Students, teachers, journalists, and readers became confused. They could no longer look up a word and find out whether it was preferred usage or substandard. It was not "all right," for example, when I was a copy editor to spell the word *alright*. It now is, according to Webster, since so many people spell it that way.

Because they wanted students to read, writers, reviewers, and editors relaxed their standards a generation ago to make literature "more relevant," something readers could "relate to." By the 1970s, the trend was to allow the first-person narrator to sound like a young person, complete with slang and grammatical errors. As an editor, I wanted the characters to sound convincing, yet I hated to perpetuate grammatical barbarisms, even though it seemed to be worth it, because the readership of young adult novels increased in schools as students saw themselves reflected on the pages.

13. *Respect other cultures.* When the dominant class in publishing was white and Protestant, unflattering stereotypes rou-

tinely appeared in books, including children's books. I enjoyed reading *The Five Chinese Brothers* and *Little Black Sambo* when I was a child and did not realize how racist the books were. The wonderful stories were not meant to be racist, but the illustrations were, and both have since been reissued with new art. Ask the person whose sex, nationality, religion, or race is being depicted whether the portrait is true or gratuitously offensive. Outsiders are often unwittingly insensitive to the feelings of certain groups.

We use *African-American*, although *black* is still accepted, and the use of *people of color* is widespread. The word *Oriental* is no longer acceptable usage for the Arab, Chinese, Japanese, Korean, Pakistani, Philippine, Vietnamese, and East Indian peoples; *Asian* is preferred since *oriental* is a Eurocentric compass direction and implies that Asians are east of London, once the capital of the British Empire.

The picture is not so clear when dealing with Native Americans, who call one another *Indians* and regard *Native American* as having been coined by guilt-struck white people. All persons of whatever race born in North, Central, or South America are *native Americans*. It is better to honor the Indians by using tribal names, like Sioux or Wampanoag or Maya, when possible.

With the dissolution of the Soviet Union and its control over other European countries, national designations have changed. People are no longer Czechoslovakian but either Czech or Slovak. Bosnians are no longer Yugoslavs; the only Yugoslavs left are Serbs and Montenegrins. It is no longer *the* Ukraine, but Ukraine. Be sure your sources are up-to-date.

14. *Write for the long term*, because your book may be in print for years and too much slang will make it seem dated. Do you remember that by the time the first President George Bush used the word *nerd* in the 1980s, young people scoffed at him? "Nobody says that anymore!" (Well, *adults* still do, but it has a specific meaning related to rich scientists.) Children have new words all the time. Use the wrong word, and your credibility as a writer for contemporary children is lost. Remember, too, that many of your readers do not recall the time when Bush was president.

Some slang has passed into the language and become almost legitimate, but when you're trying to be current, you can't know whether the latest slang will stick around, so it's best to avoid it. Lively modern writing does not depend on slang. It depends on how you use the English language.

The same idea holds true for current events, from movies to music to election campaigns. Ten or fifteen years down the line, a new generation of young people may be reading your book, and if they find it dated, it will not stay in print. If you must use a real name, when referring to contemporary culture, find one you believe will be around for a long time. Fortunately, with reruns and the rise of the VCR, classic movies and TV shows like *Babe* and the *X Files* will be enjoyed for years. But few teenagers care who Madonna or Michael Jackson are. Time moves fast in these mass-media days, so be selective.

15. *Think twice before you use a brand name* in your book, and be sure you use it correctly, because you might end up in court. For example, it's Xerox copy, not a Xerox, and it's Levi's jeans, not

simply Levis. Coke, Kleenex, Windbreaker, Polaroid, Windsurfer, Corn Flakes, Frisbee, Roller Blades, Dumpster are all trademark names and must be capitalized. If the proprietor of a good allows a lowercased product name to be used without challenging it, he can lose the trademark, which is what happened with products like kerosene. Some manufacturers are even insisting the trademark symbol (^{TM}) be used with the name, but publishers have resisted this trend. They and readers do not want to see books littered with little letters all over the pages.

Brand names are realistic, to be sure. On the other hand, books are one of the last places without ads or commercials.

16. *Eschew euphemisms*. It's not nice to call a person a fat slob; it's no more polite to call him an overweight slob. *Fat* is not an insult; it is an adjective, pejorative today, but complimentary yesterday, as in "the fat of the land," meaning prosperity. However, since Hollywood and the fashion industry have decreed that being fat is unacceptable, Bo, the narrator in Strasser's book quoted earlier, is being euphemistic, if not coy, when she describes "the grandmothers" with a medical diagnosis instead of her own opinion. She could have used another descriptive word like *dumpy* or *voluptuous*—but since she didn't use the f-word, we sense her discomfort regarding fat women. (She is fat herself, by the way.) Notice, too, that she doesn't say *old* or *middle-aged*. It would be too impolite, she thinks, too unpleasant, even though they are fat and middle-aged women. (This says more about society than it does about the women.) Bo's choice of words reflects her character, but a third-person narrator should write in standard English.

Does it matter? Yes, because as George Orwell and others have pointed out, euphemisms reflect attitudes of society. In his essay "Politics and the English Language," Orwell writes: "[The English language] becomes ugly and inaccurate because our thoughts are foolish, but the slovenliness of our language makes it easier for us to have foolish thoughts. . . . Bad habits spread by imitation."

New euphemisms turn up every day, as in the use of *home* instead of *house* in the real estate business. My sixth-grade teacher, Miss Griggs, told us that "home is where the heart is," whereas a house is only a building. Realtors, obviously, are selling fantasies of happy homes, and it seems everyone is selling a fantasy of some sort. Do not let yourself be seduced by euphemisms. You owe it to your readers because you are, after all, their teacher. The writer of serious books is an observer of humanity, a thinker, a critic.

You'll find many good books on writing at the library or bookstore, including books on usage. Most writers swear by *The Elements of Style* by William Strunk, Jr.; it's full of good advice not only from Strunk but also from E. B. White. Most copy editors and proofreaders refer to *Words into Type* or *The Chicago Manual of Style* for matters of punctuation and grammar. Writers should keep these books at the ready, to understand why copy editors, who strive for consistency and accuracy, have made changes in the manuscript.

The search for the right word, the nuances of punctuation, the ability to connote with language as well as to denote are as important as knowing what kind of flour to use when baking bread, how long to knead, how long to let the dough rise. We're used to seeing perfect loaves in the bakery. But like writers, bakers have created their share of misshapen loaves. Learn from your mistakes and go on to do your best. A book should be like a loaf of bread, tender, tasty, and nutritious under a crackling crust, something we can chew on with satisfaction.

10

Secrets from the

Carrot Patch

✦

HOW TO SUBMIT A MANUSCRIPT

A friend is a lot of things, but a critic he isn't.
—Berm Williams

"Don't you need an agent to get published?" Gus asked me. He was depressed. His novel had been returned—again. "Nobody is reading unsolicited manuscripts any longer."

"True and false," I told Gus. "Many houses no longer read unsolicited manuscripts except for those submitted by agents."

"How do I get an agent?" he asked next.

"The best way," I said, "is to sell a book to an editor."

"Very funny. You mean once it's sold, an agent will want me. Catch-22. I can't sell a book without an agent."

"False. You can still sell a manuscript over the transom."

As I told Gus, some editors, even at the most cosmodemonic houses, welcome unsolicited material, which, figuratively speaking, comes in "over the transom," a phrase coined in the days when offices had transoms, small windows above the doors. Hopeful writers would toss manuscripts through open transoms, and editors would read them. Although transoms have virtually disappeared, many publishers still handle unsolicited manuscripts (or "slush" or the "discovery pile") the traditional way. After all, the most cosmodemonic publishing house in the world could not exist were it not for the writers. Grace Clarke, the former vice president and editor in chief at the Simon & Schuster Children's Book Division, once said to me: "The writers hold the apex of an inverted pyramid in their hands. Without writers, no one in the pyramid would have a job." Reading slush is one way to find new writers.

Every day, someone from the mail room drops off stacks of manuscripts in editors' in boxes. If the editor is not accepting unsolicited manuscripts, the envelope may be returned unopened or with a form letter stating the policy. A better way to find out who does not welcome unsolicited manuscripts is to check the sources mentioned in chapter 5. The listings state which houses will read unsolicited manuscripts, and the publications keep writers up-to-date on editors who are seeking material.

Receptive editors usually have assistants who open each submission and read the cover letter and a few pages or the whole manuscript. This is called the first reading. The pile of submissions goes down quickly, because by now the assistants are fairly sure that those who write notes on stationery with pictures of puppies and kittens or those saying "my grandchildren loved the story" or those who have the word *writer* after their names are amateurs. Not always, but most of the time. The assistant will decline those manuscripts by returning them to the writers with a form letter saying something like "Thank you, but your work isn't right for our list." New writers are puzzled by this phrase and may wonder how to make the manuscript right for the list. Be bemused no longer. Phrases such as this are simply a polite way for editors to say, "We do not want your manuscript." It means nothing else. A few manuscripts will get a second reading, either from the assistant, who may write a report recommending it, or from the editor herself.

Let's assume Gus found out through networking (the best way) that Annabelle Jones, who recently joined Upstart Books, where she has her own imprint, Annabelle Jones Books, has put out a call for fiction. Annabelle used to be an executive editor at Floe, Iceberg, and Glacier, but she was fired during the restructuring after FIG merged with Newton Books and became part of Cookie Cutter Publishing Empire.

Gus sent off his novel, titled *Five by the Sea,* to Annabelle. From what he'd told me, Gus's novel sounded as if it had a chance. It was not an amateurish picture book about Octavia Octopus who fell in love with Otto Otter or a cell that wanted to be fertilized.

In spite of all his pessimistic feelings about publishing, the first week or so Gus found himself fantasizing once again about the fate of his work, as so many writers have done before and will do forever. Annabelle would begin to read his manuscript the day she received it, Gus thought, counting on his fingers. Enchanted and impressed, she'd spend the rest of the day turning the pages. "Splendid!" she'd cry at last. "This is perfect for my new list." She would telephone him before the week was out and send a contract and check a few days after that.

Instead, Gus waited. He checked the mail every day. Weeks went by, then months, then years. Surely she's had time to read it by *now*, Gus thought as he combed his beard. (He'd vowed not to shave till he sold a book, and by now he had to wrap his beard around his waist.) One snowy day, as he was contemplating applying for a job as a sidewalk Santa, he received *Five by the Sea* with a polite form letter saying it wasn't right for the Upstart list. In despair, he burned the manuscript, shaved off his beard, and took a job on an oil rig off the Alaskan coast.

Well, that's all fantasy, of course. Gus knew better than to wait so long for one editor to read his manuscript! Gus had been writing for a while, and he'd already made the classic mistakes and learned from them. He'd been to writers' conferences, had his work critiqued professionally, and a few editors had praised his writing. He'd sold two stories to a children's magazine, but so far, he hadn't sold a book.

He'd abided by the ground rules. He'd printed out his manuscript on 8 1/2-by-11-inch white bond in double-spaced Courier font, 12 point, which looks like a typewriter face and is what editors are used to reading. He could have typed the manuscript on a typewriter, but he no longer used one since word processing was so much easier. He could also have used another font, like Garamond or Times Roman, both of which are easy to read, but he certainly would not have used all italics or boldface or anything elaborate, which most editors would regard as amateurish looking. Some writers try to impress editors with fancy typesetting, but this can backfire, because type is supposed to be "invisible," not a distraction from the words on the page.

Gus then sat down, and again on plain white bond, this time with his name, address, telephone number, and date at the top, wrote a cover letter to Annabelle Jones. He mentioned in his letter that he was glad to see that she had her own imprint. As if he were writing an autobiography for a jacket flap, he told her a bit about himself, such as where he'd been educated, what kind of work he was doing—teaching is relevant to writing—and mentioned the two stories he'd published.

He also mentioned that he was sending the manuscript to two other editors. "Anyone who doesn't multiple-submit is crazy," declared Susan Hirschmann, publisher of Greenwillow Books and senior vice president of HarperCollins Children's Books, at a writers' conference. Given the long turnaround time, writers no longer can afford the luxury of sending a manuscript to one editor at a time. Most editors understand this, though not so long ago, they resented multiple submissions. Some editors still will not read multiple submissions, and it is so stated in the lists of publishers mentioned earlier. Each writer has to decide for himself which course to follow.

Gus had discovered it wasn't a good idea for him to send a manuscript to more than three editors at a time. For one, it was

✦ The Cover Letter ✦

This is the letter Gus sent accompanying his manuscript. One need not include a cover letter with a manuscript, but it's wise to do so. Here is your chance to introduce yourself, supply some credentials, and to pitch the manuscript. A manuscript without a cover letter is like a sandwich with no bread: It may be tasty, but something is missing.

GUS CASEY

P.O. BOX 236

WEST ARLINGTON, VT 05252

(802) 555-9906

March 1, 2001

Ms. Annabelle Jones

Annabelle Jones Books

Upstart Books

123 Fourth Avenue

New York, NY 10005

Dear Annabelle Jones:

Having heard you speak at several writers' conferences, for a long time I've wanted to send you my work for consideration but until recently did not have anything worth your attention.

I'm pleased now, however, to enclose my manuscript, *Five by the Sea*, a novel of 160 pages about five motherless young people left on their own in a summer cottage after their father mysteriously disappeared. Can they survive until they find out what has happened to their father?

I teach English at Hudson Community College in Vermont and have studied writing with James Purdy. This is my first full-length book, though I have had two stories for children published in *JellyBean* magazine.

I hope all is going well for you at your new imprint. I look forward to hearing from you.

Sincerely,

Gus Casey

P.S. I have also sent *Five by the Sea* to two other publishers. If either one accepts the novel, I will let you know immediately.

Enc. SASE

hard to keep track of many multiple submissions. More important, an editor would occasionally make perceptive comments about the manuscript when she returned it, and in those cases he'd revise the manuscript accordingly before sending it out again.

Sometimes, however, the comments showed a lack of understanding of what he was trying to achieve. He ignored those. It wasn't always easy for him to be sure whether an editor wanted to see the manuscript again, but he'd learned the hard way that unless she specifically asked to see it, it was pointless to send it back. Editors frequently offered comments, even when they weren't interested in buying a particular manuscript; it was an editorial reflex to be helpful.

Gus knew his work would have to sell itself, but he hoped that by showing he knew who Annabelle Jones was and by giving himself a personality, it would help his submission stand out from the rest. He also knew that obvious form letters, indicating the writer had blanketed the city, were also a bad idea.

One day, at Simon & Schuster, I was standing with another editor by the mailboxes outside our office doors. We both picked up envelopes addressed to us by name. They looked identical. We opened them together. Inside each envelope was a form letter addressed to "the editor" and a manuscript. We then peeked at a third editor's mailbox. She had the same envelope in hers. This is the wrong way to handle a multiple submission. The manuscript should go to only one editor at a publishing house at a time. Do I have to say that all three of us declined this particular manuscript?

Appearance counts. Gus had heard that a manuscript which looked gray and dog-eared, as if it had been making the rounds for years, silently doomed itself to rejection. He put the letter and his clean, freshly printed manuscript in a box to protect them and slipped the box into a Priority Mail envelope (available free from the U.S. Post Office), along with an SASE (self-addressed stamped envelope). He then prepared similar submissions to the other two editors. Priority Mail costs the same as first class for manuscripts weighing a pound or more. He could have used the special manuscript rate, but sometimes those packages are delayed in delivery. It's expensive to be a writer, printing out fresh copies of your work or having them photocopied. The postage is high, too, but this is part of the cost of doing business.

Gus noted the date on his calendar. He knew editorial staffs were underpaid and overworked, and silence meant nothing either way about the fate of his book. After two months had gone by, he was going to write to the publishers he hadn't heard from. He picked up the bulky envelopes and headed for the car. Because the packages weighed over a pound, by law he couldn't put them in the corner mailbox. He'd drop them off at the post office before heading for his job at the community college. At the rate he was going, it would be a long time before he could afford to quit. Meanwhile, he would think about a new book to write, the best way to spend his time while waiting.

Two months went by. One copy of *Five by the Sea* had come back from Editor No. 2 within thirty days with a form letter. He'd sent it to a fourth editor and made a note reminding himself to write her in two months. He wrote to Annabelle Jones and Editor No. 3 to remind them that he was waiting to hear what they thought. He desperately wanted to telephone them, but he resisted the temptation. "After all," he asked himself, "how do I know they even got my manuscript?"

Gus wished more publishers would send acknowledgment notes. He could have sent the manuscripts by certified mail, return receipt requested, but he thought that service was too expensive. He'd sent postcards in the past, asking that receipt be acknowledged, but that didn't always work. Many editors didn't open the envelopes until they were ready to read the enclosures. He comforted himself with the thought that none of his manuscripts had been lost in the mail yet. Once he'd misaddressed one, but the post office had bounced it back to him and he'd sent it out again, with the correct address this time.

His patience was rewarded. A few days later, Annabelle's assistant, Joanna, called him to say that Annabelle would like more time to consider his work. He graciously assented. He heard nothing from the third editor.

A month later, Gus wrote to him again. Gus didn't withdraw the manuscript from Editor No. 3, but he made a mental note to break the rules and call Editor No. 3 the following week. By this time, he didn't have much hope, so he sent another copy of his novel to a fifth editor and made a note to write to that one in two months if he hadn't heard anything.

The following week he called Editor No. 3 at FIG-Newton, where Annabelle used to work. It took a while to press all the buttons and be routed toward Editor No. 3. At last he got his voice mail. Gus left his message, name, and number. Voice mail! Oh, no.

From previous experience, he was sure he'd never hear from Editor No. 3. He didn't have Editor No. 3's direct line number, and he hated the thought of calling him again and pounding his way through all those buttons. Besides, many editors kept their voice mail on permanently, and Gus knew he'd never get through to them. Nor would they return his calls. He could drop Editor No. 3 a note and ask for a return of his manuscript, which is what his writer friends advised. Instead, he decided to play the same game as Editor No. 3: incommunicado. He scratched FIG-Newton off his list. A slim chance remained that someday, Editor No. 3 would find *Five by the Sea* under his bed and decide to buy it. Gus shook his head. No time for more fantasies.

He dropped a follow-up note to Editor No. 4 and one to Annabelle Jones; he still hadn't heard from her in spite of her assistant Joanna's promise over a month earlier.

Why not? Let's admit that some editors are lazy, arrogant, and unprofessional. Period. As for the others, they are swamped. Many no longer have secretaries, but assistants, who are perpetually busy doing editorial work the editors don't have time for. Assistants don't answer editors' telephones as they did in the old days; most editors place and answer their calls by themselves. When they're busy or have visitors or are on the telephone, they have to turn on voice mail. It's often easier to leave it on until they're ready to deal with calls.

More important, in addition to the disappearance of juvenile imprints like Scribners, Cobblehill, and Lothrop, editorial staffs have been cut at the cosmodemonic corporate publishing houses while the output of books per editor has increased. Some editors handle as many as fifty books a year, or one a week. Half that many is still a heavy load and not unusual. According to an article in the *New York Times* (June 29, 1998), "The work force of publishing professionals in New York, who are largely editors, has declined by 16 percent . . . according to data from the Federal Equal Employment Opportunity Commission . . . but the number of books published in the United States has surged."

Since so many top publishing executives, most of whom are not serious readers themselves, believe anyone can be an editor, editing has a low priority. But few people other than an editor know how to give the specific advice that can help a writer revise his work. An editor is like a doctor who can diagnose symptoms and prescribe a treatment when a patient complains of pain. Seasoned editors in their prime were the first to go at many of the houses. Eager but inexperienced younger people have taken their place—or no one has—and writers and their books are suffering.

Once upon a time, the editor and her immediate supervisor made the decision about whether to buy a book—except in cases where major sums of money (say, over $25,000)—were involved. Nowadays, as Jimmy Durante used to say, "Everybody wants to get into the act." In addition to the acquiring editor and editorial director, those attending the editorial meeting to discuss the purchase of books include the art director (who will present her ideas for an illustrator), the subsidiary rights director, the marketing director, the publicity director, the sales director, the financial people, and a few more middle-management staff members.

At the juvenile division of one cosmodemonic house, for example, the editorial meetings consist of more than thirty people who had—allegedly—read the manuscript under consideration and will decide whether to buy it. Before one of these meetings, the editorial director urges the editor to be "passionate" about the book under consideration. The editor, who is bookish and somewhat shy, has been overruled and undercut so often, she finds it hard to warm up to anything except hot fudge sundaes. Her quiet presentation fails to impress those attending. The art director and some of the other staff members are restless; they'd rather be back in their offices meeting the deadlines on the books already under contract. Trapped at the table, they watch in amused horror as the sales manager says the proposed book stinks and sticks his finger down his throat. Then the marketing director says books on that subject don't sell. Finally, the president of the division (the one with an M.B.A.) says the book is "a downer" and nobody will read it. (That means he didn't read past the first chapter.) Obviously, everyone's tired by now, and nobody wants to buy anything. The thirty experts decline the manuscript. Besides, it's time for lunch.

Aware of scenes like this, Jane Yolen, the writer and editor, wrote me the following:

> I am an eternal optimist about my writing, always sure that a
> better word, a bigger plot twist, the perfect character is about to
> appear. And it always does. About publishing I have no such

feeling. I expect the worst, am never surprised when it comes, and only modestly surprised when something even remotely nice happens.

Gus, however, was still optimistic about getting published. He was sure that if he persisted, he'd find an editor who admired his work. He wished he had an agent. It was tiresome keeping track of all the submissions and writing the follow-up letters. But it was early yet, he told himself. Who knew what tomorrow might bring?

11

Bunnies to the Rescue

✦

DEALING WITH AGENTS, EDITORIAL CONSULTANTS, AND EDITORS

Champions keep playing till they get it right.
—Billie Jean King

Gus knew which agent he wanted, Julia Saunders. He'd heard her speak at a writers' conference and liked her style and what she said. After the conference, he'd asked her if she'd represent him, but Julia had said she could take on only writers whose books had been published or those who'd sold a book and wanted an agent to negotiate the contract. She'd given him her card, and he was waiting for that sale so he could call her.

Wouldn't it be easier for Gus if Julia took him on? Of course. Meanwhile, who is paying Julia's salary? She is, and her income depends on selling books to publishers and taking her 15 percent commission. Although she has a respectable stable of writers whom she represents, she has to work hard for them and for her income. Of course Gus was tired of submitting his own work to so many editors and keeping track. But Julia has about twenty clients, twenty times as much confusion to contend with, and her income is only slightly higher than Gus's.

When she'd first started her agency—she'd worked in publishing many years but had been let go during a restructuring—she actively sought clients. Unfortunately, she found out that 90 percent of the manuscripts she received were like those she'd seen as a slush reader when she was younger. As Sheldon Fogelman, a lawyer and literary agent, had remarked at a writers' conference, because so many publishers had closed their doors to unsolicited manuscripts, the agents are now the ones who get the slush.

Especially vexing, Julia found, were the submissions that consisted of one picture book, the first the writer had ever written. Sometimes the hopeful writers would say they'd already submitted the manuscripts to many editors but had no luck. That's why they wanted an agent: They were confident she could place the book because of her "connections." Julia tried to maintain her professionalism when she sent the material back. (She did not return manuscripts or artwork when no SASE was enclosed.) Whether the book goes to the publisher from a writer or an agent, it still has to be publishable. An agent is not a trickster, able to transform slush into silk. Julia could not afford to take on people who had written only one (unsold) book and already exposed it to all the potential buyers.

Further, as Grace Morgan, a literary agent, once told me, the condition of many of the submissions she receives is distressing.

They often are downright messy (to be kind), full of typing errors. She also wondered why some writers, when submitting proposals, send her three nonconsecutive chapters of a manuscript. "There's no point in sending unrelated chapters," she said, "even if they are the best chapters a writer has. Writers should send the first three so I can get an idea of what they're writing about." Like all agents, Julia and Grace want serious writers, writers whom they could help build careers.

It isn't that agents don't want to encourage new writers. They know from bitter experience that even the books they admire will not pass muster with editors if they are flawed. Many editors today are looking for outstanding books that are publishable upon submission. Editors of the old school still enjoy working with writers to improve their work, but many do this only for writers whose books they've published before, not for new writers. Most other editors either do not have time or do not know how to edit!

As for agents, they simply don't have the time to edit manuscripts, read the revisions, and then send them out. Nor can reputable agents charge editing, or reading, fees without being criticized for the practice. Some agents charge fees for reading or editing, but it's wise for writers to avoid them unless they come highly recommended. On occasion, Julia had paid people to read for her, but she couldn't afford to keep that up. Anyway, agents are supposed to *sell* manuscripts, not edit them. She'd begun referring hopeful writers to freelance editorial consultants, or book doctors.

Many writers benefit from going to workshops where they receive advice from published writers and working editors, but because of time constraints and other considerations, this advice is often too general or too brief. Some writers are fortunate enough to live near a college that offers first-rate courses in writing for children. For years, writers have sought out Margaret "Bunny" Gable at the New School in New York City and profited from her thoughtful critiques of their work and from class reaction to it. (I could name a few published writers who took work already under contract to Bunny's class before they submitted it to their editors!)

For those without an appropriate school nearby, the Institute for Children's Literature (ICL) offers a correspondence course for children's writers. Each writer works with the same teacher during the course, and this close attention can result in great strides being made, especially by new writers. The teachers at ICL are usually writers themselves or former editors.

It is also possible to join or form a juvenile writers' group, where other aspiring writers offer support and suggestions. These groups vary in their usefulness. For one thing, too-kind friends hesitate to say anything negative. Blunt friends who openly declare their distaste for a manuscript crush the feelings of insecure writers. And writers themselves are not always aware of market trends and will encourage work that doesn't have a hope of being sold. Where else is a writer to turn for an objective judgment of his work?

If you're sick, you go to a doctor, who prescribes a course of treatment. If your manuscript is ailing, you can take it to a book doctor. The best way to find a good book doctor is the same as finding a good agent. Ask your friends or knowledgeable people whether they know of a reputable editorial consultant. Writers' magazines carry ads and are another source of names, but the quality of the people is impossible to judge that way. Still, if no other opportunity presents itself, you can answer those ads, being sure to stick to those who specify they have had editorial experience with juvenile books. Most editorial consultants will send you material about themselves and their fees. As you read their material, you can discover how clearly the book doctors themselves write. Is there more hyperbole than information? Do they give you a reasonable time frame for editing your work? How professional do they seem from the presentation? Do they provide reputable credentials? What do they promise to do for you? If they promise publication, be wary! Unfortunately, some editorial consultants, like some agents, are confidence men and women, promising much, relieving you of your money, and delivering nothing.

Since you are hiring your own editor, you have the right to telephone and ask questions. Again, this will give you an idea of whom you are dealing with. Editing falls into two types. The first is "structural," devoted to the "big picture," examining the strengths and weaknesses of plot, theme, characterization, pacing. Once the structure is solid, an editor might go through the manuscript again and "line edit," which is a fine-tuning, paying attention sentence by sentence to details—such as effective dialogue—with a combination of editing and rewriting. (Copyediting is yet another type of editorial procedure. However, it is done by the publisher *after* a book is under contract. A copy editor checks facts, consistency of spelling, capitalization, and punctuation, and marks up a manuscript for the printer, and her work should not be confused with line editing, though copy editors often line edit as well.)

Fees for structural and line editing vary with the book doctors, and estimates might range from $50 to $500, or possibly more, depending on the amount of work required. If, after discussing the fee with the book doctor, you regard it as too high, you can withdraw your manuscript. If the fee is satisfactory, you will likely have to pay in advance.

What should a critique consist of? The book doctor may ask the following questions: Are the characters believable and true to life? What is the conflict in the book? Does the book have a clear point of view? Does the book tell a compelling story, one that is not predictable? Do we learn something from each scene? Which scenes should be cut? A thoughtful critique will point out such problems as a faltering plotline, weak motivation, and poorly developed characters—all of which prevent a book from getting published.

As an agent, I've referred many new writers to book doctors, and the result was usually something like this: "Although the editor's comments were painful and disconcerting, he did an outstanding job of pointing out the areas that required revision and of providing suggestions for improvement. In short, his comments left me with definite insight into my writing."

Although a book doctor will suggest what might be done to strengthen a manuscript, upon reflection, a writer might come up with a different solution. According to Pamela D. Pollack, a former editor in the Simon & Schuster Children's Book Division and now the owner of an independent editorial service called Book Doctors, Ink: "The important thing is to find out where and why a story isn't working, and to do something about it. Whether or not a book doctor's advice leads to publication, it is enormously helpful to have such information. One lasting benefit is that you can apply what you have learned to other projects and use it to aid your development as a writer."

Having your own book doctor is like having your own piano teacher if you're an aspiring pianist. Even some published writers have used book doctors before sending their manuscripts to their regular editors. They want the material to be as close to perfect as possible. They are also prepared to have an editor ask them for yet another revision because different editors focus on different aspects of manuscripts, just as readers vary in their reactions.

Gus had faith in his work. He promised himself he'd follow up with Annabelle and Editor No. 4 the next day. And maybe, if Annabelle said she was returning his manuscript, he'd consult a book doctor instead of sending *Five by the Sea* to Editor No. 6.

Gus didn't have to call Annabelle. When the telephone rang the next morning, he was almost out the door on his way to work. After a moment of indecision, he picked up the receiver. It was Annabelle Jones of Upstart Books. He managed to say hello and then listened to her talk about how much she loved *Five by the Sea*. She wasn't ready to offer a contract yet, she went on, because the book had problems. Would he be willing to revise the manuscript and send it in once more?

Gus liked the sound of Annabelle's voice, but he didn't know what to say next, other than "Of course I'd be willing to take another stab at the manuscript." Then he asked, "Does this mean you want to buy the book?" He waited anxiously for her answer.

"I can't be sure now," Annabelle said. "We'd rather wait till we see the revised manuscript. We want to be certain you can make the necessary changes before we offer a contract."

Gus shook his head, then said, "I understand." But he didn't. He wondered why she was reluctant to make him an offer. He remembered hearing from experienced writer friends that editors used to buy books first, then ask for revisions.

Fortunately for Gus, Annabelle said she was returning the manuscript with an editorial letter. She didn't want to go into detail on the telephone, she said, but she wanted him to know again how much she admired his work.

Gus wanted to ask Annabelle specific questions about the manuscript, but he'd been warned by writer friends that it was a bad idea to ask for comments on the telephone. If an editor criticizes, say, the motivation of a character, the writer will reflexively defend his work and an argument could break out. Or he might find himself being so overeager that he agrees to make the change and later finds he doesn't want to. Being of the old school, Annabelle herself prefers to keep the author-editor relationship pigeonholed. The telephone is for good news, small talk, and making lunch dates.

Editorial suggestions belong in writing, she believes, especially if they are extensive. A letter spells matters out, page by page, with specifics. It becomes a record for both the editor and the writer. Often a writer needs time to absorb the news about a requested change. He can put a letter aside until he is ready to deal with it. Friends of Gus complained about getting editorial suggestions over the phone, revising the manuscript, and then being told by the forgetful editor that the changes were unnecessary! Other writers become so anxious they can remember nothing from the phone call and have to call back. Others scribble down notes so quickly they can't read them later.

On the other hand, after Gus hung up, he stared at the phone wondering what was wrong with his novel. He also wondered if he'd made a mistake, agreeing to revise without a contract. He shrugged. What choice did he have? He could withdraw the manuscript and send it elsewhere, but he'd already done that without success. At least Annabelle had mentioned the word *contract*, although it was not a sure thing. He considered informing the editors who still had not responded to his submission that Annabelle was interested in the novel. But why should he withdraw the manuscript from them? Suppose one of them made an offer ahead of Annabelle? He decided to let events take their course.

By the time he received Annabelle's letter and the edited manuscript a month later, Gus was ready to rewrite the entire book. He'd still had no word from Editors No. 3 and No. 5, and Editor No. 4 had declined the manuscript with a form letter. Gus imagined all the flaws Annabelle had found and held innumerable arguments in his head with her.

And then he read her letter. It was eight pages long, and she'd made a number of suggestions. More than anything else, she wanted him to reconsider the ages of some of the young people. Gus wasn't sure he wanted to change the ages, so he put down the letter and picked up the manuscript itself. Annabelle hadn't written much, but now and then she'd scrawled notes like "wonderful!" or "needs development" or "please clarify" in the margins. And "cut?" In spite of himself, Gus found he was caught up in her suggestions, and he began to pencil in some of the simple changes as he read and made most of the suggested deletions. Considering what he'd been thinking before he got the package, most of her suggestions would be a breeze to make, and he even wondered whether she had a valid point about changing the ages of the protagonists.

This story has a happy ending. Gus changed the ages and made the other revisions and sent in the manuscript. A month later, Annabelle called to say she wanted to buy it. She made a modest offer with a standard, she said, 10 percent royalty. This time Gus was ready. He told her to discuss the amount of the advance and the other terms of the contract with his new agent, Julia Saunders.

Before he'd begun revising, he'd been in touch with Julia and told her Annabelle was seriously interested in the novel. Julia had commiserated with him about the delay in getting a firm offer, but she said asking for revisions in advance of the contract is common practice if an editor has not previously worked with a writer. "The main thing," Julia had said, "is that she likes your book enough to want to work on it. She wants to present the best manuscript she

can to the publication board so that she'll get approval to buy it—
and that means you have to revise it first." Julia had agreed to handle the negotiations for him when Annabelle made an offer.

The time had come. Julia congratulated him on the offer and
agreed to speak to Annabelle on his behalf. She also told Gus she
was sending him a copy of her agency agreement. After being a
happy creator, Gus had now become a businessman. During the
next several days, he read over Julia's agency agreement and
showed it to a few writer friends. They told him it was standard,
similar in most respects to those they had. Some writers had no
agreements with their agents, but they'd been writing for a long
time, when a handshake sealed a deal. "It's not a ladies and gen-
tlemen's business any longer," one writer said. "It's a businessman's
business. Nobody trusts anybody, and putting terms in writing protects everybody."

Julia's agency agreement spelled out how long it would remain in effect, in this case until terminated by either party upon
ninety days' written notice to the other. The ninety days would
allow for pending submissions and other matters to be dealt
with. The agreement went on to spell out that Julia would represent *all* Gus's books—no matter who sold them, writer or
agent—but not his short stories, articles, or poetry unless agreed
to otherwise. She would also control all subsidiary rights of
books placed with a publisher either before or *after* termination
of the agency agreement. She also promised not to sell any such
rights without his agreement. Many writers don't realize that the
rights do not automatically revert to the author if the author and

agent agree to separate; the agent is still entitled to income from books she has represented.

Julia's compensation would be 15 percent for the sale of domestic or dramatic rights and 20 percent for the placement of foreign rights. The rate was higher for the latter because she had to employ subagents in foreign countries, and the higher rate covered their shares. She also expected to be reimbursed for certain expenses—such as for photocopying manuscripts and extra postage—none of which would be incurred without his permission. Unlike the established agents in big firms, Julia had no backlist of commissions to help her with office expenses.

In return, Julia would review Gus's manuscripts and assist in preparing them for submission. She would also negotiate and review all book contracts, collect and render payments in a timely fashion—usually within sixty days—and examine royalty statements. Gus had no objections, and he signed the agreement and returned it to Julia.

A few days later, Julia called Gus to tell him about the contract with Upstart Books, which she had just finished negotiating. "Annabelle would not agree to a larger advance," Julia said, "but she had agreed to an escalated royalty." She went on to explain that if *Five by the Sea* sold over 15,000 hardcover copies, the royalty would go up from 10 percent to 12-1/2 percent. Annabelle had also agreed to give Gus twenty-five free copies of his book instead of the standard ten. "Since this is your first book," Julia said, "I wasn't able to get much more for you, but you'll see the contract in a few weeks and can judge for yourself.

If there's anything you take exception to, please give me a call and we'll discuss it."

The rules may have changed, Gus realized, but the game wasn't over. He was getting his book published! It was time for some champagne. Tomorrow he would write to the editors who still had not returned his manuscript, informing them of the sale and asking that the manuscripts be returned to him in the SASEs. What a good feeling that was! He headed for the refrigerator and the bottle of champagne that had been in there since Annabelle's letter had arrived.

12

Splitting Hares

◆

CONTRACTS, COPYRIGHT, AND
WRITERS' RIGHTS

You must do the things you think you cannot do.
—Eleanor Roosevelt

Once you have an agreement with an editor, the amount of time it takes to receive a contract depends on the publishing house and the amount of bureaucracy entailed. At some houses, before an editor can get a contract for an author, she must fill out a form specifying the advance, royalty rate, number of book pages, quantity to be printed, cost of artwork, and so forth, and send it to the production department for an estimate of how much it will cost to manufacture the book. Then a business manager will take that figure and do a "profit-and-loss" analysis. (The names of these steps may differ from house to house, but the aim is the same: to find out whether it is financially feasible to publish the book.)

If the numbers work out, the editor will then fill out another form, a contract request, and give it to the editorial director for approval. If all goes well, the editorial director will then ask the publisher or president of the firm to approve the request. Finally, a month or so later (depending on whether all the principals are available), the request will reach the contracts department, where it will wait its turn to be typed. It then goes back to the editor for checking. Sometimes the typed contract circulates once again to the editorial director and publisher. One editor told me that contracts at her firm go through over thirty steps before the check due on signing is mailed, and the process takes about three months.

Luckily, being a small house, Upstart sped Gus's contract through the efficient contracts department in only a month. From there, it went to Julia, who reviewed it, negotiated a few changes, returned it to Upstart for revising, and then got it back. This time she sent four copies to Gus for his signature. Why four copies? One is for the contracts department, one for the editorial files, one for the agent, and one for the author.

Gus sat at his desk and went over the papers, clause by clause—there were forty. He stopped for a minute when he read that all monies were due and payable to Julia Saunders Literary Agency. Then he realized Julia would take out her commission and pass on the rest to him as per their agreement. This was a part of the writing game he knew little about. He had to trust Julia, but for the future, he was going to do some research on his own about contracts. He continued reading, using a ruler to keep his place as he perused the fine print.

Most of the fine print in a publisher's contract is what is called "boiler plate." It consists of standard legal protections for the publisher and spells out various percentages, amounts of money for various items, and a number of nonmonetary clauses. One such is the warranty clause, where the writer "warrants," or guarantees, that the book contains no "recipe, formula, or instruction" that may harm the user; this is especially important in books for children. Another clause asks the writer to warrant that the book contains no obscenity. Julia had told him about this one. She'd said definitions of obscenity differ so dramatically, it's best to ask that this clause be deleted. Gus saw it was crossed out on all four copies.

Gus read every word of the contract. He also had to warrant that he would not invade the privacy of a third person or state anything libelous about him. Defamation in writing is called libel; in speech it's termed slander. Because written material is often used in a spoken medium like TV, the term *defamation* is heard more often. Another reason not to use brand names, Gus thought. If he made a disparaging statement about a real product, it might result in a lawsuit.

He paused at the permissions clause. He had to pay the fees in advance of publication for material requiring permission, such as songs and poetry. He called Julia. "In advance?" he cried. "Sorry," she said, "but publishers no longer will lay out the money and deduct it from your royalties. You have to pay for everything up front. Also, when the book is published," she continued, "you can order copies at your author's discount, but you'll have to pay on delivery. Publishers are afraid they won't collect." Gus hung up the phone. He saw that even with an agent, he couldn't fight all the battles. Maybe later, when he was rich and famous. If he ever got there! At this rate, every move he made cost him money!

Under the copyright law, he knew that as a writer he owned his creation, or intellectual property. Written material copyrighted before 1978, when the current law was put into effect, was protected by copyright for twenty-eight years, with the right of renewal for another twenty-eight, for a total of a maximum of fifty-six years. The 1978 law extended the renewal term to forty-seven years, for a total of seventy-five years. More recently, in 1998, Congress voted to extend the copyright term another twenty years. Along with authors and songwriters, corporations like Disney fought to protect characters like Mickey Mouse, which was scheduled to enter the public domain in 2000. Therefore, in general, works published more than ninety-five years ago may be in the public domain; that is, they are no longer protected by copyright unless the author has been dead for fewer than seventy years. In Gus's case, his work will be protected for ninety-five years after his death.

Gus is entitled to payment for any reuse of his work. Julia had negotiated these rights, granting some to Upstart and retaining others for herself to sell. Gus decided at last that the following clauses concerned him most.

Upstart Books had bought North American English-language rights to the novel. That meant Julia was free to sell rights to the book in the rest of the world. These are known as territorial rights.

After 1992, many of the cosmodemonic publishers began to insist on buying *world* English-language rights. Foreigners owned so many American publishers that the business had become global, multinational. It made sense for a German, British, or Australian owner to have the world English-language rights to a property, and it would offer more money for them. It was more profitable for an "American" publisher to sell the books in the rest of the English-speaking world than to sell rights to a British publisher, which would then be entitled to sell English-language books in the European Economic Community because of an agreement made allowing this in 1992. Being a small, privately held publisher, Upstart worked in the traditional way. Using subagents she employed in various countries, Julia would try to sell British (English-language) and other foreign (translation) rights, and Gus would keep a larger percentage of the money received on those sales.

Gus sped over that part. He wasn't interested in global politics. Then he found what he wanted: the advance. There it was: Upstart agreed to pay $4,000 in advance of publication. The advance was split so that half would be paid on signing of the contract and the other half on delivery of an acceptable manuscript. Gus wondered about that and made a note to ask Julia for clarification. He'd already delivered a manuscript Annabelle had thought was publishable. Didn't that make it acceptable?

Gus studied the royalty schedule next: He was to receive 10 percent of the cover price of his book. He knew his $4,000 advance would come out of the royalties, so the publisher had to bring in $40,000 in retail sales before he was entitled to receive any more money. He did some quick arithmetic. If his book sold for $15.00, he would receive $1.50 per copy; the publisher would then have to sell 2,667 copies before the advance was "earned out" and he would receive more money. This deal, he knew, was preferable to receiving a percentage of the "amount received" by the publisher. The amount received is often based on half the cover price, because of discounts to various buyers. Buried in the contract were other royalty amounts based on different kinds of sales, such as export sales, special sales, book club sales, and so on.

Julia was aware of those, but most were boiler plate items she didn't regard as important enough to dispute. She had tried to rework the "book fair" special-sales clause, where the amount the author received was based on a small percentage of the amount received by the publisher. A writer could see 25,000 copies of his book sold to a book fair enterprise and then receive only a little over $1,000 himself. Annabelle had refused to change the clause because publishers rarely make much money on these deals either. Julia told Gus she had no way of getting more money for him in this case.

An important part of the juvenile market, book fair sales—and other special sales—are made with the understanding that the books are not returnable. It is a cash sale, so to speak, and favorable reduced royalty terms are extended to firms like Scholastic and Troll, among others, which run book fairs on a national level. The firms buy large quantities and put their own prices on their editions' covers. Local book fairs also discount the cover prices of books, but the royalty may not change. Book fairs are usually held in schools, where books, mostly paperbacks, are sold to the children themselves at bargain prices. This system works to everyone's advantage, it is said, because the children can afford to buy their own books, and it's a way for an author to begin building word-of-mouth publicity. Gus wondered why the author has to pay for this kind of publicity, then suppressed the thought. He continued reading.

Julia and Annabelle had worked out how income from the various subsidiary rights would be divided between the publisher and the author. Subsidiary rights include the following: *British publication*, in English, including the EEC; *foreign-language translations*; *trade paperback*; *mass-market paperback*; *first serial*, publication in magazines and newspapers (before the book is published); *second serial*, publication in periodicals (after the book is published); *textbook*; *large print*; *anthologies*; *book club*; *performance* (motion pictures, plays, TV, radio, etc.); *computer software*; *electronic*; and "all other rights not specifically mentioned."

The income from sales of subsidiary rights is divided between the publisher and the author, and the "splits" vary. Unlike most of the cosmodemonic publishers, Upstart Books does not have its own mass-market paperback line, so the subsidiary rights manager will try to sell those rights to one of the houses that does. Upstart will divide the income with Gus, who will get 60 percent of the amount. If one of the cosmodemonic houses had bought *Five by the Sea*, it would have offered a "hard/soft deal," meaning it would have paid a higher advance to get the rights to the mass-market paperback. Gus would also have kept all the royalty income because he would not be sharing it with Upstart or another publisher.

As it turned out, that would be the case with the trade paper-back edition. Upstart could publish *Five by the Sea* as a trade pa-perback and pay Gus a 7 percent royalty. Gus wondered about that 7 percent. He called Julia and asked for an explanation. "You mean," Gus said, "that by changing the quality of the cardboard used for the cover, Upstart gets away with paying me a 7 percent royalty? The inside is exactly the same as the hardcover edition." Julia agreed that the trade paper royalty was low, but publishers' margins on paperbacks are also low, because the retail price is less while it still costs a substantial amount for paper, printing, and binding; less money is made per book. Perhaps at a future date she might get him 8 percent, but 7 percent was a good rate these days, Julia said. Many publishers were paying only 6 percent. One edi-tor she knew had refused to go up to 8 on another contract, saying it was "giving up the store."

Gus found himself getting more bewildered as he read through the contract. He found the reversion-of-rights clause, which he'd heard was important. If his book went out of print, and another publisher wanted to reissue it, he had to have the rights returned to him by the original publisher before he could publish the book elsewhere. Some publishers will not revert rights if any edition is in print anywhere. Gus saw that Upstart had modified this clause so that it referred only to English-language rights. He also noted that a typewritten addition said Upstart had up to three years to sell the various rights; after that, they reverted to him. Gus was glad he had an agent, but he vowed to read up on contracts and pay closer attention at writers' conferences to the contract negotiation seminars. Someday his contracts would be even more complicated and the advances larger (he hoped). He wanted to be prepared for that.

What should a writer do who has no agent? Some writers seek out their family attorneys, but this isn't always a good idea because publishing law is a specialty that's not completely understood by people who practice other forms of law. Still, a writer may feel more comfortable having a lawyer's advice, as she would before signing any contract. For a fee, attorneys who deal in publishing law will read and negotiate a contract for a writer. Some professional groups like the National Writers Union (NWU), and the American Society of Journalists and Authors (ASJA) offer contract training sessions. The Society of Children's Book Writers and Illustrators has an informative brochure about contracts, and a number of books on the subject are available. A writer can also ask colleagues for their recommendations, keeping in mind that since she is dealing with a reputable, established publisher, the firm is not out to cheat her, legally speaking. Naturally, the publisher wants the best deal possible, and so does the author. But the author also needs publishing credits, so this is not the time to be striking a blow for writers' rights, except, perhaps, in the following cases.

For the last decade or so, publishers have included one or more clauses relating to electronic rights in contracts. This is a complex and controversial issue. (Keep in mind that dramatic or *perfor-*

mance rights for movies and TV are included separately in the list of subsidiary rights and do not constitute "electronic rights" as used here.)

As publishers grew bigger, many formed their own divisions to handle audio (tape recordings) and computer disk versions of the material under contract. This, obviously, is a growing and lucrative field. Because of mergers and acquisitions, the cosmodemonic houses include divisions that can exploit the rights acquired in the editorial departments. They call this "synergy," and as a phenomenon it has had varying degrees of success within the corporations.

An "electronic version" means any method of copying a work (or a portion of it)—whether as a recording, for storage in a database, retrieval, broadcast, or any other transmission—that uses an electronic, electromagnetic, analog, or digital signal. This includes, but is not limited to, magnetic tape, floppy disks, laser disks, integrated circuit chips, CD-ROM, and methods not yet devised! In short, your book might end up on a CD-ROM. Bill Gates's book, *The Road Ahead,* came with a CD-ROM tucked into it, for example. That CD-ROM was probably an exercise of the electronic rights granted to the publisher—which Bill Gates, being heavily invested in the software business, is eager to see happen more often.

Since so much entertainment is stored electronically on tape, disk, and CD-ROM, electronic rights can be a gold mine for the proprietor, and writers and agents must defend their right to negotiate electronic rights. Several years ago, Random House, for example, declared that electronic rights are not negotiable; they must remain with the publisher. As a consequence, a number of writers, including Julia Child and Jacques Pepin, left Random House. Other publishers either split the rights fifty-fifty or say they will "negotiate them in good faith" when the time comes to sell those rights. If a publisher insists on retaining electronic rights, the latter is probably the best way to proceed for now. Even better is for the author or agent to retain the rights, though most authors do not know where or how to sell those rights to their best advantage.

The right to photocopy a work is not included in most book publishing contracts, but the ease and low cost of photocopying and scanning led to professional concern about this particular electronic right. First, writers learned that their work was often illegally copied for use in classrooms and other public places. Then, as periodicals went on-line, writers discovered their works were made accessible to viewers on the Internet through various providers. The NWU, ASJA, the Authors Guild, and other writers' organizations immediately cried "Foul!" Through the united efforts of these organizations and literary agencies, the copyright law was enforced so that photocopiers would pay fees for the right to make copies of written works for corporations, schools, universities, and others. The Authors Registry was formed to handle the licensing and bookkeeping for nearly every important writers' group and almost one hundred literary agencies, whose members and clients total more than fifty thousand. The Registry collects and pays out the accumulated amounts for photocopy and electronic use. For the first time, writers are seeing income from the photocopying of their material.

The struggle for equity in regard to on-line electronic rights has also had success. The president of the NWU, Jonathan Tasini, and six other writers sued the *New York Times* and others because the *Times* would not pay freelance writers fees for the use of their articles in its on-line version of the paper. Tasini and the other writers lost the case in 1998, but it was appealed, and in September 1999, the Second Court of Appeals reversed the federal district court decision—to the joy of all writers, and especially to those who write for magazines and newspapers. The new ruling stated that the reuse of freelance work on databases (such as Nexis) and CD-ROMs without the author's express permission constitutes copyright infringement. Also, both parties must sign a contract granting permission for additional uses of material. However, that is not the end of the story. The *New York Times* has since taken the case to the U.S. Supreme Court for a final opinion.

Writers are fortunate that their agents and organizations are fighting for an equitable distribution of monies. Electronic publishing is such a new area that it's safe to say many don't understand it yet. It is all the more important for writers to band together in organizations that will look out for them and to remain current by reading newsletters, newspapers, and other professional material. The ASJA has a free on-line service called Contracts Watch (www.asja.org), which keeps a running document on electronic and other rights. In one article, Alexandra Cantor Owens, executive director of ASJA, pointed out, for example, that Bantam Books was changing its standard offer for a *Star Trek* TV tie-in novel from advance-plus-royalties to flat fee. This led to protests by writers and writers' organizations. Such battles go on all the time, and writers must remain vigilant or else they will become simply vendors and not creators of valuable and original intellectual property.

The writer or artist remains the creator, the source, of material that publishers and filmmakers desperately desire. Intellectual properties are among the major exports of the United States. Consider how much income Shakespeare's works still generate—and he's been dead for centuries! It's unfortunate that his heirs do not benefit from this, but the fact that intellectual property comes into the public domain eventually enriches readers (and publishers) while it impoverishes the heirs.

In future struggles, writers' organizations and literary agents will be on the side of the authors, and it's in the interest of all writers to support them. It is also in the long-term interest of publishers, Owens said, because "when talented, skillful, authoritative, professional writers encounter deteriorating work conditions and diminished career prospects, they move on. . . . Chasing away the most reliable providers of content is a dumb way to grow a business that relies on content."

So, writer, be aware!

13

The Tail End

✦

True ease in writing
comes from art, not chance,
As those move easiest
who have learned to dance. —*Alexander Pope*

After the contract for *Five by the Sea* had been signed, Gus did one more revision for Annabelle and received the second half of his advance, which was due on the delivery of an acceptable manuscript. This is a time-honored practice, where the publisher delays payment until the editor is satisfied the author has made all the required revisions. Gus had read that *acceptable* can be an ambiguous term, but, in essence, it means that the editor judges the manuscript to be satisfactory.

Meanwhile, Gus had begun to work on another book, a biography of E. B. White, the author of *Charlotte's Web* and other books for children and adults. Before starting to work, he had gone to the library and checked *Children's Books in Print*, which lists books by title, author, and subject. He checked the library database and found no listing of a juvenile book on White. Nor had he seen any mention of one in any of the publishers' catalogs he'd read on the Internet. It seemed the field was clear, so after he'd done his research, he'd written a summary, an outline, and three chapters and turned them over to his agent, Julia Saunders. As a courtesy, Julia had already offered the book to Annabelle, who had declined it since her firm did little or no nonfiction. Gus wanted to keep up his writing momentum, but he wasn't sure whether he should finish the E. B. White biography before it was sold or work on a new novel.

Gus had faith in the E. B. White idea, and he wanted to continue with his research and writing while he was still enthusiastic. When (not if) the book was sold, he thought, he'd be that much farther ahead with it. He'd already asked Annabelle if Upstart would be interested in a new novel, but she'd said Upstart couldn't take on another book from him until they'd seen how the first one sold.

Gus was puzzled. Wasn't he supposed to be "building a career"? He telephoned Julia and asked her advice. "Publishers are reluctant to take risks on unknown or little-known writers these days," she said. "Put aside the E. B. White manuscript and work on a new novel. I can only sell finished novels," she told him. "Meanwhile, the White proposal is in shape for submitting, so we should send it out now."

Gus took a long walk and pondered the advice he'd received. He wanted to write and get published. He'd had one book accepted by a publisher who didn't seem eager to have a second one from him. His agent had told him to write that second book anyway. Although she was sending the nonfiction book out, she wasn't all that excited about it. Was he supposed to spend the next year writing a book that no one might want?

Julia's advice was consistent with that from agent George Nicholson, who told me that the best way for a new writer to build a career is to set limits on what he wants to publish.

Hopeful writers send me samples of all their work, from picture books to encyclopedic nonfiction works. I tell them to concentrate on one genre and become so good at it that I can place their work with a publisher. Once they've become established, they can work in other genres.

I have given up sending out picture books for writers and suggest they do it themselves. The market is tight, and marketing picture books is too time-consuming for me with my small staff. I will negotiate any sales, of course, because it's my job to protect the writer and get her a good contract.

It's also probably a good idea for a writer to have more than one publisher, but each publisher should focus on one kind of book. For a prolific writer, it would be ideal to have one house to do picture books, another nonfiction, and a third for fiction exclusively.

The writer must write whether her books sell or not. She

must also take responsibility for her career, because as an agent I
can only recommend an action, not enforce it.

At Upstart Books, meanwhile, it was time to put the *Five by the Sea* manuscript into production. Like most writers, Gus was unaware of what happens at a publishing house after it deems a manuscript acceptable. The wheels have begun rolling, and people are getting into gear to work on the manuscript and see it through a long, unwieldy process that takes about nine months for the finished book to be produced.

Although it's true that most houses request manuscripts on disk, some hardcover houses still follow the traditional practice of working directly from hard copy—or, as it still is called, a manuscript. The writer should check his contract to see exactly what the publisher expects. Most houses want a disk and a manuscript. A word count for the entire book printed on the title page can be useful, and a character count for each chapter will be even more useful, but it's not necessary for the writer to furnish this information.

After Gus turned in his third revision, Annabelle read it, lead pencil in hand. She made a few comments here and there, corrected some spelling, and asked a few questions, which Gus could answer later on in the publishing process. She was pleased with the manuscript. Gus was a good writer, and she was glad to have him on her list.

The steps that follow are essentially the same for all kinds of books. Picture books have an added step in that the art is proofed, and the color proofs corrected, during the production process. Writers do not get involved in this stage, but some top-selling illustrators may be invited to watch the book on press and make color adjustments.

While the book was fresh in her memory, Annabelle drafted selling copy. She had learned this was the best time to write the copy that would be the basis for all the written material about the book which would appear during its lifetime, in the publisher's catalog, on jacket flaps, in fact sheets to be distributed to other departments, and possibly in ads—if there were any. Sometimes lazy reviewers reprinted the flap copy, hoping to pass it off as a review. Annabelle smiled. That was so good for the book when it happened!

Using the present tense and keeping proper names to a minimum, she finished summarizing the plot. Then she considered her final paragraph. Publishers used the same adjectives over and over, and she tried not to use the same ones twice on the same list. She remembered the time, years ago, when someone had proposed taping up a sheet of paper so editors and assistants could declare dibs on the adjectives they'd used in the current season's copy; no one else would be allowed to use an adjective on the list. *Moving* was always good, as was *poignant*. Maybe *touching*? She reached for her dictionary of synonyms, perused the entries (*pathetic*? no! *affecting*? too vague), and settled on *moving*.

Since *Five by the Sea* is a young adult, or teen, novel, for readers over twelve, it will not have interior art. Had it been a middle-grade book, the art director might have suggested possible illustrators to do six or eight black-and-white drawings and the jacket. After a brief conference with Annabelle, one would have been selected. Illustrators often receive a portion of the royalties, usually 1 or 2 percent. This is negotiated at the time the book is signed up, and authors receive lower royalties as a consequence.

Annabelle instructed Joanna, her assistant, to transmit *Five by the Sea* to production, and in a note gave Joanna the information she would need for the transmittal form. This included an estimate of how many pages the book would run; the trim size (the size of the page); the kind of binding; the quantity to be printed and bound; the publication date; and other details. She also summarized the plot in two sentences and suggested how the book should look—she wanted it to have a serious and contemporary appearance, which matched the text.

She asked Joanna to write copy about the author, based on the biographical questionnaire Gus had returned with the contract several months earlier. Joanna had kept a copy of the questionnaire on file and sent the original, along with the photo of himself Gus had provided, to the publicity department. Staff members would refer to it when writing biographical copy for their own purposes.

Joanna got to work on *Five by the Sea*. Luckily, all concerned were satisfied with this title. Otherwise, production would be held up until a final title was chosen because the front matter could not be prepared or a jacket assigned to an artist. Joanna found the biographical questionnaire and wrote Gus's bio. Since this was Gus's first book, she emphasized his hometown, his education, and where he lived now. These are selling points for the book; publishers hope sentiment will cause booksellers to order books based on where the author might have friends or colleagues interested in buying his book.

Joanna then retyped Annabelle's draft of the copy into the proper format for the jacket, which included the price, the ISBN number (see below), age and grade codes, the publisher's name and address, and the line required by law, "Printed in the U.S.A." She gave it to Annabelle for perusal, along with the bio. If Annabelle was satisfied, the flap copy would go to the editorial director for her approval.

Joanna went on to prepare the front matter for the book, which included a half title, title page, copyright, and dedication. When the author has titled the chapters, a contents page is also included, which Joanna would prepare if the author had neglected to do it. Front matter for a nonfiction book may be more elaborate. All editors and designers refer to the *Chicago Manual*, *Words into Type*, or *Bookmaking* when they have questions about the order in which the various components should appear.

In general, the first page is the half title: the title of the book—no subtitle, no author, no publisher. Years ago, booksellers would stack unbound books in their shops and identify them by the half titles, which also protected the insides of the books from being damaged. Customers would take the books elsewhere for binding.

Page 2 is usually a blank or it may be an "ad card" (a list of other books by the same author in chronological order). If it contains an illustration or map, it is called a frontispiece.

Facing the second page is the title page, which carries the *official* title (and subtitle, if there is one) of the book, the names of the author and illustrator, and the name and location of the publisher.

The copyright page comes next, on the reverse, or verso, of the title page. The book contract specifies the name in which the book will be copyrighted, and writers must make sure it's specified properly when they review their contracts. In addition to the copyright notice and a statement "reserving all rights," the copyright page carries the full address of the publisher, a line indicating the edition, and the Library of Congress Cataloging in Publication (CIP) notice. The CIP is prepared at the Library of Congress and is the official catalog card used in the Library of Congress and at many other libraries. The Dewey decimal system number is also on the card.

The ISBN, or International Standard Book Number, appears on the copyright page as well. This is the order number, which was assigned to the book when the contract was final. The first digit is usually 0, which stands for "English language"; the next three or four indicate the publisher; the next group is the number of the book itself; and the last is a checking number. The title and copyright pages are like an identity card; each book must have one for legal protection as well as identification.

Sometimes the name of the book designer appears on the copyright page—often the only person other than the author and illustrator who takes credit for her work. Editors of hardcover books remain anonymous by tradition, as do all the other people who have made the book possible. Were a list of credits to be published in the book, it would not be so long as those on movies from Hollywood, but it would be substantial—especially if it included the delivery person from the local coffee shop.

If there's enough room, the dedication will appear on the first right-hand page after the copyright notice. Again, "Everybody wants to get into the act," but this time it's the writers who sometimes go overboard on the dedication page, remembering every person they've ever known, perhaps afraid they'll never have a chance to dedicate a book to someone again! Books come from a clerical and aristocratic tradition, where restraint is favored, and that applies to the dedication.

If the book has chapter titles, a table of contents, which should be prepared by the writer, comes on the next right-hand page. Sometimes a writer will want to open his book with a quotation, or epigraph. It goes on a right-hand page after the dedication, if space permits, with the contents page afterward.

A second half title or a part title may appear before the text proper begins. Part titles are necessary when a book is broken into parts; for example, "Part One: The Family Together." If there's no part title, a second half title can be inserted if the designer needs to fill a page. Designers choose a typeface and calculate the size, number of lines per page, and so on to ensure that all the pages will be utilized, leaving no blanks, or pages without type, at the front or back of the book.

In a nonfiction book, there may be other matter, such as a preface, foreword, author's note, or introduction. A preface is often an aside on the text itself, perhaps discussing research methods or giving thanks to people who helped with the book. This is the place to thank people, instead of on the dedication page. Or a brief acknowledgments page can be inserted. Both of these elements may come before the contents page; if they do they should not be listed in the contents. A foreword is an essay written by someone other than the author, perhaps to lend credibility to the book or to elucidate it in some way. An introduction is by the author and is an integral part of the text.

The front matter is sometimes numbered with Roman numerals, which are usually not printed in novels, though they can be seen in textbooks. If there's a part title, the two pages before the first text page are Arabic number 1 and Arabic number 2, because by tradition a part title and verso are considered part of the text. In some books, the counting begins with Arabic numerals in the front matter, so that the first page of text might carry a folio (page number) reading 7 or 9.

The term *back matter* applies primarily to nonfiction, and the contents page might list the following as part of the back matter: appendix, glossary, source notes, bibliography, and, last of all, the index, because it is not prepared until the page proof stage of the production process.

The short biography of the author and illustrator at the end of the book is not considered an integral part of the book—the author did not write it; the editor did. It carries no page number and is not listed in the contents.

After Annabelle and the editorial director approved the flap copy and bio, Joanna retyped the bio, this time with the heading "About the Author." She placed it at the end of the manuscript, with a blank piece of paper behind it for protection. Manuscripts take a beating as they make their way through the production process. Many people handle them, and the last page, if not shielded, gets dirty and torn. Joanna added the author's photo and photo credit to the bundle and gave it to Annabelle for a last look. All the necessary pieces were in place. Annabelle and Joanna triumphantly passed on the manuscript and a duplicate copy to the next person who would handle it, the managing editor.

If there is one person who knows everything in an editorial department, it is the managing editor. Although the duties vary at each publishing house, usually the managing editor is in charge of trafficking the manuscript; that is, she makes sure the manuscript and the ancillary parts are complete and then sends it on to the different departments that will work on it, in this case the copyediting and design departments. The managing editor keeps track of the schedule and deadlines and makes sure each person does his part on time. Once a week she chairs a production meeting, where editors, assistants, art director, designers, copy editors, and others convene to discuss the schedules for the various books.

While the original manuscript is being copyedited, a designer will begin her work with the duplicate.

The chief of copyediting decided to send *Five by the Sea* to a freelance copy editor, Allen Gale. Allen works at home, where he has a small but thorough collection of reference books. He refers to them often while working on the manuscript and flap copy. Allen is a graduate of a well-known university, where he majored in Latin, of all things. He loves facts and is a storehouse of information. He had once astounded everyone at a meeting where a rebus book was discussed. *"Rebus,"* he'd said, "is the ablative plural of the Latin *res*, or 'thing.'" Allen had taught for a while, but teaching didn't suit him because he preferred to work alone. Copyediting makes use of his education and knowledge, and he feels part of a noble tradition. He's also a crackerjack speller. As he works, he keeps an alphabetical list of proper names and unusual spellings on a separate piece of paper called a style sheet, which will later go to the proofreader for his reference. Allen will also rewrite ungrammatical passages, correct misspellings, and revise punctuation so it conforms to house style.

English grammar and spelling keep changing, but the style should be uniform in a given book. Therefore, each publisher has a list of house rules, and the copy editor ensures that the book conforms to it. For example, some houses prefer the serial comma—the comma before *and* in a list of items, as in: "baseball, bat, and glove"—and others don't use it. Years ago, "closed" punctuation was favored; today an "open" style is preferred, with fewer punctuation marks, especially after short adverbial phrases at the beginnings of sentences. A house rule may dictate that commas be inserted only if the phrase is longer than five words—or eight.

Spellings can be tricky as well, especially of ordinary words, which is why copy editors use the latest edition of the dictionary. Not so long ago *backseat* and *backyard* were each two words; the spelling checker on my word processor says *backseat* is still two words, but Webster's tenth edition says it's one, as is *backyard*. Would anyone but a copy editor notice that in Leo Tolstoy's *War and Peace* (translated by Constance Garnett) *cannonball* is sometimes one word, sometimes two? They didn't have style sheets in those days, but custom today dictates that inconsistent spelling, typographical errors, and misspellings that may distract the reader must not pass uncorrected.

Copy editors are also supposed to doubt all facts in a book and to check each one. Sometimes the simplest, most obvious errors occur, as when I copyedited a picture book that mentioned "President Stonewall Jackson" and left it that way. It is not a good idea to cut costs by having the person who copyedited a book proofread it; errors are perpetuated. Luckily, one of the sales reps caught the gaffe while the book was still in proofs, and the error was fixed. The author had made the mistake, and the editor and copy editor hadn't noticed because it *seemed* correct; type lends legitimacy. Much more serious is the error that makes its way into a finished book—and then into a review. Some reviewers pay more attention to errors than to content and will effectively kill a book with too many errors in it.

✦ Frequently Used Proofreader's Marks ✦

Editors, copy editors, and proofreaders use the following marks to indicate changes to be made in a manuscript or proof. Changes in a manuscript are written directly in the body of the text, while the proofreader's written changes go in the margins of the proofs, with marks placed in the text to indicate where the changes are to be made. Editors use pencil—not pen—because nobody's perfect, and the other people use different colors to indicate which person suggested the changes. Authors should also use pencil.

OK /⟨?⟩	Query to author; i.e., is this change all right with you?
stet	Leave the material as written (dots placed under words show which material is meant)
ℐ	Delete (a letter, word, phrase, sentence)
Cap	a̲, set as capital letter(s)
lc	A̸, set as lowercase letter(s)
⟨Feb.⟩	Word (or number) should be spelled out
#	Add space (either between words or lines)
∧	Insert a word, phrase, letter, etc., here
ital	Set underlined material in <u>italic</u> type
rom	Set circled material in ⟨roman⟩ type
⊙	Set a period
⟨	Set a comma

$\frac{1}{M}$	Set a one-em dash (the width of the letter M)
$\frac{1}{N}$	Set a one-en dash (half the width of a one-em dash, used to indicate a range of numbers or dates, as in 1863$\frac{1}{N}$1901)
=	Set a hyphen, as in jewel-like
¶	Begin a new paragraph here
run in	Run text together without a paragraph break

A more complete list of marks can be found in most dictionaries.

As he works, Allen uses proofreader's marks on the manuscript because it is the language publishers and printers use to convey instructions precisely. It's easy enough to learn, and writers should teach themselves the basic marks so they'll understand the changes made in their copyedited manuscripts. Allen writes directly in the body of the text when he makes his corrections in brown pencil and puts his queries on colored slips of paper attached to the manuscript.

When Allen completed his work on *Five by the Sea*, he sent the manuscript back to the chief of copyediting, who forwarded it to Annabelle. She reviewed it a final time and asked Joanna to send it to the author. Gus was given two weeks to answer Annabelle's final editorial queries as well as the copy editor's. Annabelle had asked him to use a colored pencil (not brown) and to strike through (not erase) any changes he didn't agree with, and to answer editorial queries on the colored slips of paper, which he should not tear off. He didn't have to agree to every suggestion. *The book is, ultimately, the author's work, and he has the final word, even when he's wrong.* This is known as poetic license. One best-selling writer wanted the sun to set in the Atlantic Ocean east of Long Island, and no argument would persuade her to change it.

According to *Dear Genius: The Letters of Ursula Nordstrom*, collected and edited by Leonard S. Marcus, Nordstrom handled a change she wanted to make in the galleys for *The Sign on Rosie's Door* (1960) by writing to Maurice Sendak:

> *I had an idea about that one line "Everybody shook their heads yes"—which was the one that we left even though it wasn't grammatical. I tried to call you . . . to ask would it be OK with you if we changed it to "Everybody nodded." That means everybody shook their heads yes but it will protect you and your book and your ever-loving cotton-picking publishers from being ostracised by the English teachers of this here great and gorgeous country with its locked-in goodness. Well, since I couldn't get you on the phone I made this slight change but if it sends you screaming out into the street we can go back to the other.*

Nordstrom was in a hurry to get those galleys back to the production department because the book was on a schedule and all deadlines had to be met. Each deadline involves many people: The compositor has scheduled a time to set the type for the book, and far off in the distance, the bookbinder is waiting. Some houses do composition on their own computers in the production department, but schedules are still important. After Gus returned the copyedited manuscript, it would take a few more weeks before he saw the next stage of production, galley proofs.

Meanwhile, in the art department, the art director, who assigns books to freelance illustrators and supervises the design staff, had given the duplicate manuscript to a book designer for a *cast off*, or *character count*. The average children's novel of 160 pages may contain over a quarter of a million characters. (A character is each letter, numeral, space, or punctuation mark in the manuscript.) The designer chose an appropriate typeface and size to fill the number of pages Annabelle had asked for.

In some houses, the display type for the title page and chapter headings will not be selected until after the jacket art is in. Ideally, the display type on the jacket, which complements the artwork, is used inside the book as well for a uniform, custom appearance. Other houses work more quickly and don't care whether the jacket type and title page type are the same.

To make sure that the book will look attractive, the designer may ask the compositor, the person who sets the type, to provide sample layouts showing how the chapter openings and text pages will look in the chosen typeface. Annabelle and the designer studied the layouts and sample pages to be sure the size of the type and the number of lines per page were right for the age of the reader. The younger the reader, for example, the larger the type and the fewer lines of type per page. The book was running long. Annabelle and the designer discussed the possibility of subtracting two pages from the front matter by printing the dedication on the copyright page. The alternative was to add more pages to the book (which would make it more expensive because of the extra paper) or use smaller type or less "leading" (the spaces between the lines).

When Annabelle was satisfied with the layouts, the designer marked up the copyedited manuscript with the type specifications. These specifications include such details as how much space should be left between the top of the page and the first line of each chapter ("sinkage"), how wide the margins and gutters (the center margin between the pages) should be, where the folios should be placed, the style of the running heads (or feet) on each page, and much more. (Running heads appear at the top of the pages, usually with the author's name or part title on the left-hand page and the book title or the chapter title on the right; when they are at the bottoms of pages, they are called running feet.) Printer's jargon is colorful and steeped in tradition. *Widows*, for example, are partial lines of type at the top of a page, and good bookmakers frown on them. *Orphans* are single words at the bottom of the page. Type can be adjusted to kill the widows and orphans.

Finally, the manuscript was ready for the production department to take charge. These are the people who select the printer and purchase the paper for all the books. An enormous amount of material flows through their department as they traffic manuscripts and all stages of proofs back and forth between compositors, printers, binders, and the editorial and design staff. If Gus's book went into a second printing, they would handle that too.

Five by the Sea went to the compositor at last. A few weeks later, the galleys arrived. (Technically speaking, these were not true galley proofs, which are long sheets of paper, not yet broken into pages. With computer typesetting, it's possible for the compositor to supply proofs broken into pages. These are called first pass by some, galleys by traditionalists.) The proofs were distributed to staff members, including Annabelle. She sent a set to Gus and asked him to return it in two weeks. She reminded him that this was the last chance he'd have to see his book in type before it was printed. He was allowed 10 percent of the composition cost as an allowance to pay for any further corrections; if he exceeded that amount, he'd be charged.

Gus didn't know exactly how many corrections he was allowed, but he was more concerned with publishing a good book than with money. Still, he worked carefully and kept the changes to a minimum. He was surprised at how authoritative his words looked now that they were in type. It also struck him that he'd read the book so often, it seemed boring. Was it any good? he wondered.

Meanwhile, the copyediting chief had sent the master, or main, set to a freelance proofreader, who would read it while comparing it to the original manuscript. Proofreaders mark each correction as either a printer's error, PE, or an editorial alteration,

EA, when the change is the result of a lapse in the editing or copyediting.

The proofread galleys went back to Annabelle, who had Joanna transfer Gus's changes to the master set, marking each one as an author alteration, or AA. Later, the printer would count up the AAs, and if Gus had exceeded his allowance, the amount would be deducted on his first royalty statement.

Over the next months, Annabelle and Joanna would be checking three more stages of proof: second pass (formerly called page proof); repros (reproduction proof, printed on coated paper so it can be photographed); and blues, or blueprints, made from the film to be used to print the book.

The blues come from the printer and are folded into book pages. This is the first time anyone has seen how the finished book will look as a unit. This step is especially important for illustrated books, since artwork or photographs and captions are in place along with the display type for the chapter headings. The house proofreader checks the blues not only for PEs but to see that all the pages are there and in the right order.

The blues go back to the printer. He exposes the film to a flexible metal sheet, which is treated with chemicals and placed on cylinders within the press. The entire book is printed quickly on immense sheets of paper. They go to the bookbinder by truck, where they are folded and gathered into signatures, or groups of pages, and then trimmed. The pages are sewn together and glued into cases, or bindings, which are usually made of thick cardboard covered with cloth and paper. (Paperbacks are not sewn but only glued into stiff paper covers.) Each book then gets dressed in a new jacket, which is folded and put on the books by hand.

The jacket had arrived at the bookbinder by a different route from the rest of the book, but work on it had begun months ago, at about the same time as the manuscript for *Five by the Sea* went into production. The jacket has its own schedule because it is printed at a different place from the text. Annabelle needed the jacket proofs for the sales conferences, and the deadlines were tight. (In the paperback world, cover proofs are needed at least six months before the books are shipped from the warehouse.)

Gus, of course, had no idea of the activity that had been going on at the publishing house during these months. His proposal for the E. B. White book was still making the rounds, and he'd been working on the second novel as Julia had advised him to do. He was thrilled when Annabelle at last sent him a copy of the finished book, and he sat down to examine it. Good jacket, intelligent flap copy, flattering photo of himself. He began to read the book. "Not bad, not bad at all," he said.

In her office, Annabelle opened a copy of *Five by the Sea* and stood it on a bookshelf next to the other titles on the current list.

"Terrific jacket," Joanna said.

Annabelle nodded and went back to her desk and picked up a manuscript. "This one is ready for production. Would you do the transmittal?" She handed the manuscript to Joanna.

"This business is never boring, is it?" Joanna said.

"Each book, each writer, each journey to publication is different," said Annabelle. "When we start publishing books as if they were as interchangeable as potato chips, then the game will be over." She sat down. "Meanwhile, we're lucky to be publishing children's books the old-fashioned way. With hard work and love."

14

Bunny Goes to Market

✦

PUBLICITY AND PROMOTION

Courage is very important. Like a muscle, it is
strengthened by use. —Ruth Gordon

Gus was not aware of all the marketing that had taken place well before he held the finished copy of his book. As you may remember, Annabelle, his editor, had written selling copy for the catalog months earlier, when she'd transmitted *Five by the Sea* to production. Versions of this copy were used on the jacket flap and on the fact, or tip, sheets, which would be given to the sales reps when the book was discussed at the sales conferences in the months ahead.

After the selling copy had been written, work began on the jacket for the book. The dust jacket (for hardcovers) or cover (for paperbacks) is not the writer's responsibility but the publisher's. The publisher can put whatever it likes on the jacket or cover, because a jacket not only protects the book but is an advertisement for it, thus part of the marketing program. The artwork lends value to the book and is often copyrighted separately from the text. According to a 1998 survey cosponsored by *Publishers Weekly* and BookExpo America, fifty-seven out of one hundred teenage book buyers said the book jacket is the single greatest influence on their choice of a book.

Once all the manuscripts were in production, Annabelle and the other editors, the art director, assistants, and designers attended a meeting to discuss the jackets for the current list. Before the meeting, Joanna, Annabelle's assistant, had gone through yet another duplicate copy of Gus's manuscript to look for scenes that might be illustrated. Her criteria included showing the principal characters in action that reflected the theme and spirit of the book. She and Annabelle discussed the six possibilities for *Five by the Sea* and chose three to present to the art director.

Hardcover editors favor jackets that reflect the theme of a book, while paperback editors want high action and emotion appealing to readers' fantasies. For example, the hardcover jacket art for *The Night Swimmers* by Betsy Byars showed a pensive young girl, with two boys (her brothers) and a swimming pool in the distance behind her, and, on the verso, a seated man playing a guitar. Painted by Troy Howell, it suited the book perfectly. The book was about a motherless girl whose insouciant country singer father had put her in charge of her younger brothers, who were causing difficulties too serious for her to handle. The swimming pool belonged to the man next door. When the jacket was shown to the reps at the presales conference, they screamed,

"Downer!" "Change it!" In those days, editors prevailed over sales and marketing people, so the jacket remained as it was. The editors were therefore doubly pleased when the book with the downer jacket won the American Book Award in 1981. When the paperback came out, the cover emphasized cheerful children at a swimming pool. That cover was also a fair, if incomplete, representation of the story, but it emphasized good times over sad times, in the mistaken belief that children don't like to read sad books. Howell's interior art was preserved, but, obviously, the cover no longer matched his style. This often happens because the paperback world demands covers with an instant appeal for the mass-market rack.

At the jacket meeting where Gus's book was discussed, editors and the art director talked over ideas and selected the scenes to feature. After the meeting, Joanna typed up a jacket request for *Five by the Sea,* including copyedited copy for the title, author, ISBN, et cetera, and then provided a duplicate manuscript for the jacket artist to read. She described the desired scenes in detail and highlighted the manuscript pages to which the artist would need to refer. Some artists read the manuscripts, and some don't. Some prefer to choose their own scenes, and some prefer to work from prescribed ones. Practices differ at different houses, but however the jacket art is done, it will be Annabelle's responsibility to approve the art and Joanna's job to check the sketches to be sure all the details are correct. Sometimes a sketch will be sent to the author; often it is not. Usually, the first the author sees of the jacket for his book is the proof.

A writer may dislike the jacket art for his book because it doesn't match his mental image of the scene and characters. But an artist is hired to do an artistic interpretation that will entice a reader to pick up the book. If Gus, an unknown writer, hates the art, there's not much he or his agent can do about it. Long ago, at Crowell-Collier Press, when I was fussing over the type layout on a jacket proof and asked that it be changed, Janet Schulman, the vice president, asked, "Will it sell one more copy of the book if we spend the money to make that change?" I had to agree the change was not worth the cost. In the years to come, I kept that question in mind and asked it of myself—and others—for the rest of my career.

However, if a serious *editorial* error has occurred, the writer should insist it be corrected. Once, for example, the jacket flap for a novel said that the protagonist was seeing a *psychiatrist*. The author telephoned immediately to say no, the protagonist was seeing a *psychologist*. That was a relatively simple error to correct because it involved setting only a few lines of type and correcting the black plate. (Jackets are printed in four colors, and each color has its own "plate," which, when combined with the other three—red, yellow, and blue—gives the illusion of full color.)

Another time an author had described the protagonist as having short, curly red hair, but the artist had painted her with long, curly black hair. The author insisted on having the art changed. The artist, however, refused to correct the hairstyle unless the publisher paid him to hire another model. (He also said the girl looked better with long hair!) The publisher, who had to pay for making four new color plates, said it could not absorb the cost of a model as well. The artist finally agreed to paint over the black with red, so that the heroine ended up with rusty long hair. The author was so angry she wrote an article, which appeared in a writers' magazine, complaining that the publisher had not been sensitive to her book. In truth, the editorial department had supported her wish, but it was the production department, art director, and artist who'd dug in their heels because of the cost.

I never felt the same about that writer afterward because she saw me as her foe, not her ally. Yes, it was a stupid mistake on the artist's part. No one likes such mistakes, but sometimes the inevitable has to be accepted with grace. For the long term, authors and editors must strive to preserve a harmonious relationship, even though they will often disagree. Editors do their best to accommodate writers, but circumstances often make it impossible to satisfy everyone. Fortunately, Gus was happy with the jacket on his book.

Another factor influencing a purchase is the title. Imagine a reader walking into a bookstore or library where she sees hundreds and thousands of books. How does she select one? An attractive jacket may catch her eye, and she'll pick up the book and read the flap copy. If that intrigues her, she may read a page or two and decide the book is right for her to buy or take out of the library.

In other cases, the first thing she sees may be the spine, with only the title and author's name. Author recognition is important, because if a reader enjoyed a book by a particular writer, she's likely to want to read other books by him. If the writer is unknown, the title may invite a potential reader to pick up a particular book. I remember being fascinated as a child by a book title I pronounced "nerby," wondering what it meant. I took down the book and read a few pages, then put it back on the shelf. The title was actually *Nearby*, and the book itself didn't interest me.

Writing in the *Boston Globe*, Diane White suggested the best-seller of all best-sellers in the year 2000 would be *Golf Your Way to Fat-Free Fitness the Feng Shui Way with Harry Potter's Cat*. This would be a good crossover title, working in the juvenile as well as the adult market. The standard industry joke used to be that the most commercial title would include the words *doctor*, *dog*, and *Lincoln*. As far as I know, no one has ever written *Abraham Lincoln's Doctor's Dog*, although George Edward Stanley's *The Dog That Collected Baseball Cards* is in the right tradition. Two of my favorite children's titles are *The Celery Stalks at Midnight* and *The Girl of the Limberlost*, both of which, like "nerby," piqued my curiosity.

Not too long ago, it became trendy to put grades in titles, following the success of Judy Blume's *Tales of a Fourth-Grade Nothing*. Booksellers found it easy to sell books to aunts and uncles who wanted books for children in particular grades. Like all trends, this one faded, too, when so many "grade" books crowded the shelves that readers got bored.

When the title lacks spark and the author is unknown, the jacket illustration is triply important as a selling tool. Ideally, a book should have a memorable illustration that will appeal to everybody—sales reps, librarians, reviewers, booksellers, parents, and (let us not forget), the young prospective readers—which is not so easy to do as it sounds. Also ideally, the book should always be displayed face out so that this marvelous jacket is visible to all. Writers (and some editors) have been known to go into bookstores and libraries and shamelessly rearrange the shelves so that certain titles are face out instead of spine out. (Just don't get caught!)

The jacket proof for Gus's book was ready by the time the sales conference began, about four months before publication day. Most houses have presales conferences, where key staff members get a preview of the upcoming lists in all the divisions of the company. Sometimes a jacket meets with stiff resistance here and is changed before the actual sales conference. Once long ago, at Viking, an adult sports book for women showed a woman in a T-shirt, but only between her neck and waist. The women sales reps objected, and the male art director shook his head. "I thought it was a great concept," he said. A new jacket was ready for the sales conference six weeks later.

At the large companies, the sales conference lasts about a week and is often held at an out-of-town resort so the reps and head office staff can relax. Smaller companies will hold their con-ferences either at the home office or at a local hotel. The atmos-phere is casual but businesslike. All the reps attend and listen to the editors present the new lists.

Months earlier, Annabelle and Joanna had written the tip sheet, full of information about Gus and his book. Accompanied by full-color photos of the jackets, the tip sheets for all the new books had been collected in a massive loose-leaf notebook that was handed out to each sales rep as part of the sales kit. Bound galleys of the books and color proofs of picture books were also in the sales kit, along with the publisher's catalog and other promotional material.

When it was her turn to speak at the conference, Annabelle enthusiastically presented the books she was responsible for. The reps made notes on their tip sheets while she spoke, keeping one eye on slides of the jackets, which were projected on a screen in front of the audience. This was the first time most of the reps had heard of Gus's book.

The marketing people then explained the marketing plans for all the books. At some publishers, these plans include ads, author tours, posters, bookmarks, and other giveaways. Children's publishers have small advertising and promotion budgets, so most new books get only a mention in list ads in the professional media. Later, at dinner, the reps and editors discussed the books and got to know one another.

As soon as the conference was over, the reps would go to their sales territories all over the United States and Canada, where they'd call on wholesalers and individual bookstores. A rep has only a short time to present a long list of books to each prospective buyer, and the stores do not buy every book on a publisher's list. By the time the rep gets around to the children's books, the buyer may limit herself to picture books and the occasional hardcover novel by a best-selling writer. Those stores that have separate children's buyers will be more adventurous. The wholesalers take copies of almost everything, since they supply libraries as well as stores.

In the last ten years, publishers have had to give special attention to the buyers for the superstore chains like Barnes & Noble and Borders, who place big orders when they like a book and no order at all when they don't. The chain stores are especially important to the success of picture books and "merchandise" books—those that come with a doll or game or are watered-down texts of classics such as the Little House books. They buy hardcover novels only by Newbery Medal winners and a handful of best-selling juvenile writers.

As publication day approached, like most new writers, Gus was surprised to find out how little promotional help Upstart was giving his book. When he asked his editor, Annabelle Jones, about the advertising budget, she laughed. "Budget? There's no advertising budget." She explained that after his book appeared in the catalog and in a few list ads (buried among two dozen other titles) in professional media, that was it for print advertising, except for reviews. Upstart was generous with review copies; it sent 500 copies of each book to reviewers and library systems around the country. That was in addition to the select list of influential reviewers who'd received preliminary bound galleys well before publication date. Some publishers send only selected titles to the majority of reviewers, promoting the books they think will sell the best; therefore many books never even get to the reviewer's desk. (This is apparently a cost-cutting measure.) The only way for a writer to know whether his book went to a specific reviewer is to ask the marketing department.

Leonard Marcus, a contributing editor and book reviewer for

Parenting magazine, told me that some writers personally send him their books for review, which he regards as a waste of time and money. He reads all the publishers' catalogs—especially from small presses—and will request a book that interests him if the publisher has failed to send it to him. More often than not, he's already received a copy from the publisher, so nothing is gained for the writer. If a writer tells Marcus how wonderful the book is, that doesn't help, because as a reviewer he makes up his own mind. "That's my job," he said.

> *There's a difference between making someone a victim of a bad review and being honest about whether the writer achieved his purpose. The reviewer is charged with the responsibility of giving his reasons for his opinions. In that way the reviewer can be judged by the reader, which makes it fair. Nothing gives me more pleasure than to discover a new writer or illustrator and to call attention to his work.*

The reviews Annabelle and Joanna sent Gus were favorable for the most part. Some media, like *Horn Book* and *Booklist*, review only books they recommend, preferring not to run unfavorable reviews. Some review almost every book published, and one reviewer of Gus's book was especially cruel. Gus wanted to write to the reviewer, but Julia, his agent, dissuaded him. "You'll only alienate that reviewer if you complain," she said. "Let it go." Gus let it go, but he never forgot the nasty words of that review.

Then Gus received a pleasant surprise that (almost) made up for the nasty review. The Upstart publicity department had sent *Five by the Sea* to award committees all over the country, most especially to the state library or reading associations that award state prizes. Groups in Iowa, Utah, Tennessee, and other states draw up master lists of books for the children in their states to read and vote on. *Five by the Sea* was selected for the Texas master list, as a potential winner of the Bluebonnet Award. Not only was this a boost to Gus's ego, but it meant substantial sales, since every school library in Texas had to buy the book for the children to read.

The marketing department also sent *Five by the Sea* to many other groups for consideration. Some of the best-known accolades a book can receive are the ones from the American Library Association such as the Newbery Medal, the Caldecott Medal, a Notable Book Award, or Best Book for Young Adults award. Others include the Coretta Scott King Award, the National Book Award, the *Boston Globe-Horn Book* Award, the SCBWI Golden Kite Award, the Christopher Award, a *New York Times* Ten Best-Illustrated Children's Books Award, and to be included on the *School Library Journal's* "Best Books" list. The New York Public Library recommends books in its annual Books for the Teen-Age selection and 100 Books for Reading and Sharing list. The National Council of Social Studies and the National Council of Teachers of English also single out books for awards. Each award lends prestige to a book and puts its title out in front of prospective buyers, especially school and public libraries.

After reviews, the most important promotion a book can receive is to be featured at one of the many professional conferences held in the United States and other countries. The most important of these for a juvenile writer is the American Library Association (ALA), which holds a working meeting in January (midwinter) and a mammoth annual conference at the end of June, where as many as fifteen thousand people may attend. The American Booksellers' BookExpo America (BEA) holds its meeting for booksellers around Memorial Day. Other important conferences are held during the year by such groups as the International Reading Association (IRA), which holds meetings in the United States and abroad in May and also has state meetings for teachers; the National Council of Teachers of English (NCTE) in November; and state meetings of local library associations, such as, in April, the Texas Library Association (TLA) and, in September, the New England Library Association (NELA). The Children's Book Fair in Bologna, Italy, in April presents an opportunity to sell rights to foreign publishers, as does the autumn Frankfurt Book Fair in Germany, where the foreign rights to American books are sold to foreign publishers.

Whether it's a book fair held in Europe or a BEA, ALA, or a state library association conference, publishers set up booths. Books are on display, and representatives from the publishers stand and talk with potential buyers, showing off the wares. A potential buyer may come up and ask for a certain type of book, and the publisher's rep will show him what she has.

Held at convention centers in cities like Atlanta, Chicago,

Dallas, Los Angeles, New Orleans, New York, Philadelphia, San Francisco, or Washington, the ALA conferences feature aisles full of booths of books and library equipment, from computers to furniture. The exhibition floor is open to the public for a moderate charge. If a writer can attend an ALA conference, he will find it of immense interest and value.

Librarians representing major library systems and small ones dutifully go from booth to booth, examining the new books on display. Publishers provide tons of giveaways having to do with the new books, from author biographies and bookmarks to posters and shopping bags—and sometimes free paperbacks and advance copies of new hardcover titles. Authors and illustrators stand or sit behind tables to autograph their new books, which are available for purchase at a discount. In some cases the lines have hundreds of people; in others, the publishers' representatives invite passersby to meet the signer, especially when the signer is a virtually unknown author.

A great deal of entertaining takes place, especially of authors and illustrators with the members of the various award-giving committees of the ALA, such as the Newbery, Caldecott, Notable Book, and the Young Adult Services Division committees. This gives publishers and librarians (many of whom head state or municipal library systems) a chance to talk about books and authors in relaxed surroundings.

Although it is smaller, the midwinter ALA conference is as important as the summer one. Throughout the year, committee members have been reading and discussing the new books. At the conferences, they get together to go over the lists and make preliminary nominations for the prizes. But it's at midwinter that final decisions are reached and editors told the results. The editors of prizewinning books race for the telephones to call their authors or illustrators with the news, sometimes at four in the morning.

Winning any award makes the publisher and the author happy. It will also influence sales by bringing the book to the attention of people, which may be the first step to a bigger award for another book by that author later. The Newbery and Caldecott Medals are formally presented at a gala dinner during the summer ALA conference.

Even without winning an award, a writer may begin to get invitations to speak at schools or before library groups or other writers. As time goes on, her fame grows, and she can begin to ask for fees ranging from as little as $50 to $1,000 or more. Many writers have enhanced their careers substantially—and their incomes—by going on the road.

Another joy for the writer is to receive mail, especially from children. Some receive so much mail, they need a secretary to handle it. Others ask publicity departments to send back a form letter, especially to children who are writing and asking for information for a book report. The most common questions children ask are: "How much money do you make?" and "How long did it take you to write the book?" Have your answers ready. It's a great honor to receive a personal letter from a child.

Unfortunately, a number of self-styled moral guardians are also liable to write regarding material they consider offensive, material ranging from the use of street language to "controversial" subject matter, usually dealing with sex or religion. In addition, during the last thirty years or so, hundreds of local, state, and national groups descended on schools and libraries nationwide, demanding that certain books be banned.

It is easy to forget that literature *should* show the truth about people and life. Let us not forget what Leo Tolstoy said: "If a country has a great writer—this is like having another government." Artists have a valuable, unique vision of reality that is often at odds with community standards. If your book is attacked, get in touch with your editor. She will lend you moral support and suggest ways you can get help from various organizations, including the Committee on Intellectual Freedom of the ALA and the National Coalition against Censorship. As a writer, you *must* get involved in protecting your First Amendment rights, or we will all lose them. If the case against your book is made public, you're ahead of the game, because most people are against self-appointed censors. And you won't be alone. Every September the ALA holds its "Banned Book Week," when books for adults and children that have been censored are displayed in libraries around the country. It's worth taking a look at the display and trying to figure out why a particular book was banned.

Gus didn't want his book to get the kind of attention a banned book gets. On the other hand, he did want it to get *some* attention. He brought up the matter the next time he attended his writers' group. The members agreed that publisher publicity was virtually useless, other than in getting reviews. "You've got to do it yourself," one writer said, and she gave him some tips. Others joined in, and before he knew it, Gus had a marketing plan, which will be described in the next chapter.

15

Who Needs a Rabbit's Foot?

◆

WHAT YOU CAN DO TO MARKET YOUR BOOK

Mañana is often the busiest day of the week.
—Spanish proverb

I t's not so easy for Peter Rabbit to get into Mr. McGregor's garden any longer, as we've seen. While Peter stares at his foot, wondering what to do, remember the adage "You make your own luck." It's never too early to start thinking about what you can do to promote your book. The word *publish* derives from *publicare,* "to make public," and having a manuscript accepted for publication is only part of the endeavor; it is vitally important to tell the world the book exists.

While you were still writing, you should have been compos-
ing a list of individuals, media contacts, and key personnel at organizations who might have a special interest in reading your
book, especially if it's nonfiction or fiction dealing with a topic
that would be of interest to them. Don't overlook neighborhood
"throwaway" papers and even newspapers in places you mentioned in your book. The publisher will send your book for review to the standard media such as *Booklist*, the *School Library
Journal*, *Horn Book*, the *New York Times*, and other major newspapers. You can help the publisher by finding media that are less
well known.

Around the time you sign the contract, your editor will send
you a printed form to fill out. This is the publisher's biographical
questionnaire. If you did not get one, ask your editor to send a
copy. This is probably the most important part of your marketing
plan, and you can fill in some of the answers even before you finish your manuscript and arrange to have your picture taken.

✦ The Biographical Questionnaire ✦

Your publisher will send you a biographical questionnaire
similar to the one that Upstart Books sends to its authors
(see below). Make a photocopy of the questionnaire from
your publisher, fill in what corresponds to Section A below,
and return it with your contract or soon thereafter. This is
the information that will appear on the jacket flap or tip

sheet. (By the way, you don't have to supply the year of your birth if you'd rather not.) Tell your editor that you will send in Section B later.

During the next few months, research the information you will need for Section B. The publicity department will not look up names, addresses, and telephone numbers for you! This research is time-consuming, but it will ensure that news of your book—or copies of the book—will get to people who can help you promote it. When you are finished, fill in Section B and send it to your editor for forwarding to the publicity department.

Upstart Books: Biographical Questionnaire

SECTION A

Author's Name: Date:

Title of Book:

Home address and phone:

Business address and phone:

Date and place of birth: citizenship:

Schools attended/degrees (with dates):

Titles of previous books (including publishers and publication dates):

Honors and awards received:

Besides writing or illustrating, what other work have you done or are you doing now?

Other places you have lived or traveled:

Your interests, activities, hobbies, pets:

Describe your book, mentioning points to emphasize in promotion.

Let us know about books that are comparable or competitive with yours.

Who is the audience for this book?

How did you come to write this book? An anecdote about the process of writing it might be used in promotion.

SECTION B

Please list prominent people (scholars, reviewers, well-known professionals) who might be helpful in promoting your book. Please indicate with an asterisk those you know personally and include addresses.

Please provide names and addresses of organizations or associations of which you are a member or which you feel will have a special interest in your book.

Copies of your book will be sent to children's book review media and to periodicals that will reach readers interested in your subject. Please list professional periodicals, college papers, alumni magazines, special-interest media, and local newspapers that should also receive information on your book, with address and name of contact person if possible.

Please list localities where you are known and where local publicity might be arranged.

Please provide names and addresses of your local bookstores (please mark with an asterisk those where you are known personally).

Please list names and addresses of local libraries and librarians.

Are you available for radio, TV, or press interviews if the opportunity arises (yes/no)?

Will you speak to audiences of children (yes/no)? Adults (yes/no)? Large groups (yes/no)? Small groups (yes/no)?

If you have speaking engagements planned for the next six months, please list them, mentioning date, place, and contact.

You don't need a formal studio photograph, but you should always provide your publisher with a photo showing you as you would like to be perceived. Ask friends with good cameras to take lots of pictures of you. You don't have to go so far as some adult novelists do and dress in costumes that match the books! The effect of the pose you select should be relaxed and personal, yet dignified. The photo I sent my publisher when *Boats for Bedtime* was published had boats in the background, for example. On the other hand, try to avoid showing a blackboard or classroom behind you, unless you want young readers to see you as a teacher. When you send the photograph to your publisher, include the photographer's name as a credit. The photograph may or may not appear on the finished book; picture books almost never have author or illustrator photos. Your publisher needs to have a good photograph to give to various people along the publicity trail.

Important people—including writers, of course—may provide advance praise for your book. When you submit your final manuscript, you should give likely names *and addresses* to your editor, who will send out a manuscript early on in the publishing process for comments that can be used in catalog copy, ads, and on jacket proofs.

Although marketing plays an important role in the publishing process, many marketing departments are low on staff, especially for the grunt work. Someone has to type all those labels, insert books into padded bags, and see they get mailed to library acquisition departments and reviewers. One library promotion manager I knew told me she did all this work herself because she did not have an assistant. This is not unusual. Therefore, the marketing people can give the writer only limited help. Whatever a writer can do to aid the marketing department will be considered and done if possible, beginning with sending your book out to the right people.

Every writer needs a printed biography. Gus found out that most publishers provide biographical brochures only for their "A" authors—the ones whose books they've been publishing the longest or are the best selling. Now that the questionnaire had helped him organize his personal information, he wrote his autobiography. Pretending he was the publicist and using the third person he wrote: "As one of five children, Gus Casey has long wanted to write about the dynamics of a large family." It felt strange at first to write about himself, but it became easier and even enjoyable as he wrote about his favorite subject.

Writers can pick up complimentary author bios at conferences and use them as prototypes or can ask their publisher to send samples from its files. Everyone enjoys reading why a person wrote a particular book, so be sure to include that story in your bio. If you or a friend are proficient with desktop publishing, print out this bio with a photograph of yourself. At the least, do a "quick and dirty" bio—a photocopy on colored paper of your typed version. It will come in handy. If you have a Web site, be sure to include the address on the bio. If you are uncomfortable about supplying your home address and telephone number to strangers, have all your mail sent to your publisher or agent for forwarding to you. As for providing your E-mail address, that's up to you.

When you have either bound galleys (which many publishers use as review copies), a jacket proof—ask your editor if you can have extra copies—the printed catalog, or folded and gathered sheets of a picture book, you can visit your local bookstores and libraries to show them the material and introduce yourself. At that time you can drop off one of your bios or just a photocopy of the page featuring your book in the catalog. If this is your first book, don't expect an invitation to sign books at the store. You are not yet a draw. You might nevertheless offer to sign copies of your book later for the store to have on hand. Many bookstores have special bins for autographed copies.

Libraries also welcome authors who offer to sign copies already on the shelves. If you plan to travel to another part of the country, mention it to the publicist. It may be possible for her to arrange school or library visits at your destination. Even if she doesn't, it's exhilarating to drop into a library or bookstore in a far-off city and find your books there. Take the time to chat with the staff, who will usually be delighted to meet you.

Another possibility is to arrange an "event," which librarians, store owners, or event managers would support, once the book is published. (It is pointless to tout your book to the public before bookstores have copies; the public has a short memory.) You could, for example, suggest reading your picture book aloud during a story hour and give away autographed bios as souvenirs. People love freebies. One writer went to the expense of printing book-marks she had designed. The bookmark contained an illustration, some text, and information about where her book might be obtained. If you are an illustrator, you could draw pictures and present them—or copies—to the audience. If your book is nonfiction, you could do a short talk on the subject and invite questions and answers from the audience.

At bookstores, the idea is to sell your books, so a pile of them should be handily displayed with a store employee to help the buyers. Don't be disappointed if the books don't fly out the store or the number of people requesting your autograph is small. That is to be expected. Remain gracious and friendly, without holding up the line (if there is one). Open the book to the title page and ask to whom the book should be inscribed; then add a greeting, your signature, and date. Look up, smile, and make eye contact. A few seconds of closeness means a great deal to your readers.

It is not good form for a writer to sell her own books; that is, handle the money. If necessary, press a friend into service for you. It's part of the image. A writer also should not carry her books or boxes of them where people can see her. Consider yourself a presence, a personage, not a cashier or messenger!

Always maintain a healthy supply of your books in the trunk of your car or in an extra suitcase. It doesn't hurt to create a couple of small posters, each featuring a jacket proof and your name, in case your sponsor forgets to provide a suitable announcement. One poster should be for the tabletop where you will be signing or standing. The other is for tacking up (with low-tack tape or push-pins, which you also have in your suitcase).

One morning long ago, as I walked up Madison Avenue from the subway to my office at the Viking Press, I spotted a book on display in the window of a custom tailor. Curious, I took a closer look. That was the first time I saw the children's classic, *A Day No Pigs Would Die* by Robert Newton Peck. At that time Peck was working in advertising and was probably a customer of that tailor. How many other people walking up Madison Avenue—the heart of advertising country—saw Peck's book? If you know of any local merchants who'd be happy to have your book on display, don't hesitate to offer them an autographed copy for that purpose. They are not to sell the book—after all, bookstores don't sell clothes— but simply to show it off for a few months, after which it is their property. I carry a copy of my latest book on the dashboard of my car to be seen wherever I go. Publicity is precious!

See whether your publisher will agree to printing an order form or flyer for your book—or do it yourself with the publisher's approval. You can distribute these among your acquaintances and set them out at writers' conferences so that people will have an easy time of getting your book directly from your publisher. The piece of paper will later remind them of your book, and they'll have all the necessary ordering information, including the correct title and spelling of your name.

Family members expect free copies from you, so it may not be a bad idea to let them have an order form, too. You must let them know, gracefully, that you have to pay for the books once your supply of author's copies is gone. Depending on your relationships with different family members, you can also express the hope that they will get a copy of the book from their local bookstore.

A dear friend of mine in Virginia bought a copy of *Boats for Bedtime* through her children's bookstore. The owner had not known about the book. She ordered a dozen or so and displayed them face out. Later, she told my friend that the book was selling well, especially to people looking for books for boys. There is nothing like the personal touch.

Dozens of writers have supplemented their incomes with school visits and other presentations. In addition to your author bio, print up a brochure about your availability for school visits. Sometimes the invitation to speak comes via your publisher, but you can seek out opportunities yourself as well. Stay on good terms with your publisher's publicity department. For example, be sure to notify the staff six weeks in advance of a speaking engagement you have set up so that they may inform local media and book-stores of your appearance and to ensure books will be available for you to sign. Even so, books may not arrive in time, so in an emer-gency—only—you can use the supply you bring with you. Ac-cording to some contracts, you are not supposed to sell your own books, especially at a discount. But what is a writer to do when, for whatever reason, the books don't arrive? It's better to be prepared for this contingency than to sit and moan.

If you've not spoken in public before, learn how to. The more public speaking you do, the easier it gets. Practice on friends and family, then approach local schools and libraries and offer to speak or read your work. While you are learning, the experience is worth more than a speaker's fee. It should not be long, however, before you begin to charge for travel expenses and finally, for speaking. In my own experience, speaking at a nearby school takes at least three days out of my work life. The first is the day I prepare my program. The second is the day of the speech. The third day is re-covery. Consider this when you set your fees, which should be on a sliding scale from, say, $100 to $3,000 if you are famous. Your writer friends or the publicity associate at your publisher will help you set a fee schedule. Many schools have funds to pay for speak-ers, and it's only just that you be paid.

Finally, a great number of writers have their own Web sites.

You can hire someone to design and build one for you, or you can try your hand at creating your own, using software you can buy. The Web site should provide some information about you and perhaps some samples from your book. While your book is in print, be sure to mention your publisher and its marketing department as the source for services such as review copies and public appearances. This is what they do best, and you may find that trying to handle this on your own will be overwhelming. So that a potential buyer can order the book directly, include the name and address of your publisher, its toll-free order number, the ISBN, and price.

Before your book is out of print (OP) and rights have reverted to you, your publisher will give you the opportunity to buy up surplus copies at a generous discount. Once the book is officially OP, you can advertise and sell your book through your Web site. You will be responsible for warehousing, bookkeeping, shipping, and handling. Some companies on-line offer to handle OP books for authors for a commission.

To my delight, when I visited Powell's bookstore in Portland, Oregon, copies of my OP books were listed on the store computer. Powell's, and other stores, buy used books and shelve them cheek-by-jowl with virgin copies, so the buyer often has a choice of editions.

As long as your book is available to purchasers, keep looking for opportunities to present it. How many times have I watched a breaking news event and known of a book I'd edited that would be relevant. If you're the author of such a book, send it immediately, with a letter, to a newspaper, magazine, or other possible source that would welcome it. You might even manage to get a speaking engagement if you show such initiative. It doesn't matter whether you make money from these efforts. You are building a career, and keeping your name and your work, even if it's out of print, in front of the public is vital.

The great American poet Emily Dickinson (1830–86) once wrote, "There is no frigate like a book / To take us lands away. . . . [it is a] chariot that bears a human soul." But of her two thousand poems, only two were published in her lifetime. Today, in this information age, any writer can see her work published in some form. It is through publication that our human souls will sail on to readers today and to future generations. Books make thoughts, feelings, and stories permanent. They are small and can travel anywhere. They are one of the miracles of humanity, for only people can write and read books. They are also essential to a civilized, advanced society. Tyrants and reactionaries attack books and ideas before they attack people—a society "without a head," as the writer Edward Fenton once said, is easy to subjugate.

Over 3 billion books are printed each year in the United States, and almost four thousand titles are juvenile books. Therefore, if you want to write—and publish—books for children, the opportunities are there, and the rewards can be enormous. Many firms still operate with grace and culture, so you will be treated well if you are lucky. Research the market, do your networking, and present your work as professionally as possible.

A number of children's book publishers have come into existence since 1995 to publish the books the cosmodemonic firms won't touch. This number will increase. Just as fast-food restaurants did not cause the demise of family-owned restaurants, the cosmodemonic publishers will never be the only game in town. Small firms can make enough money to survive. The big firms are top-heavy, especially in the high-priced executive suites, where big salaries do not guarantee success for anyone for long. Innovative, successful books are coming from the smallest publishers, imprints, and packagers. Keep up with your research and target the new houses for your work.

It's easy to feel depressed or cynical about the children's market today, but if, like Gus, you want to write for children—and have talent—you will get your work published because there are still editors and houses who want good books that will sell reasonably well. Greed hasn't won, not by a long shot.

A while ago, I attended a program in the library at a local school. On the shelves I saw many old friends, books I'd edited, artwork I'd chosen, copy I'd written. It was a good feeling. And then I heard a dozen children give reports based on books they'd read. That was an even better feeling.

Writing is a lonely, painful, frustrating occupation. It may or may not earn you enough money to live on. Yet we persist because human beings are creative animals who want to transmit ideas. As George Frideric Handel said after the first London performance of *Messiah* in 1743, "I should be sorry . . . if I have only succeeded in entertaining them; I wished to make them better."

Important Addresses

ORGANIZATIONS

American Book Producers Association
160 Fifth Avenue
New York, NY 10010
www.abpaonline.org

The Children's Book Council
12 West Thirty-seventh Street, 2nd floor
New York, NY 10018
www.cbcbooks.org

Committee on Intellectual Freedom
American Library Association
50 East Huron Street
Chicago, IL 60611
www.ala.org/alaorg/oif/if/brochure.html

Institute of Children's Literature
93 Long Ridge Road
West Redding, CT 06896-0812
www.childrenswriter.com

National Coalition Against Censorship
275 Seventh Avenue
New York, NY 10001
www.ncac.org

National Writers Union
National Office
13 University Place
New York, NY 10003
www.nwu.org

Society of Children's Book Writers & Illustrators
8271 Beverly Boulevard
Los Angeles, CA 90048
www.scbwi.org

PUBLICATIONS

Booklist
50 East Huron Street
Chicago, IL 60611
www.ala.org/booklist/index.html

Appendix: Important Addresses

The Horn Book
14 Beacon Street
Boston, MA 02108
www.hbook.com

Publishers Weekly
245 West Seventeenth Street
New York, NY 10011
www.publishersweekly.com

School Library Journal
245 West Seventeenth Street
New York, NY 10011
www.slj.com

The Writer
120 Boylston Street
Boston, MA 02116
www.channel1.com/the writer

Writer's Digest
1507 Dana Avenue
Cincinnati, OH 45207
www.writersdigest.com

SUGGESTIONS FOR FURTHER READING

The following list is by no means a complete one, but it will serve as an introduction to literature, publishing, and writing for children. Many of the titles below have their own lists of suggested books.

Aldiss, Brian W., with David Wingrove. *Trillion Year Spree: The History of Science Fiction.* New York: Atheneum, 1986; Avon Books, 1988.

Applebaum, Judith. *How to Get Happily Published.* New York: Harper Perennial, 1998.

Applebaum, Judith, and Florence Janovic. *The Writer's Workbook: A Full and Friendly Guide to Boosting Your Book's Sales.* Wainscott, N.Y.: Pushcart Press, 1991.

Benét, William Rose, et al., eds. *Benét's Reader's Encyclopedia.* 3d ed. New York: Harper & Row, 1987.

Burack, Sylvia K., ed. *The Writer's Handbook.* Boston: The Writer, 1999.

Cart, Michael. *From Romance to Realism: Fifty Years of Growth and Change in Young Adult Literature.* New York: HarperCollins, 1996.

The Chicago Manual of Style: For Writers, Editors, and Publishers. Chicago: University of Chicago Press, 1993.

Cooke, Alistair, ed. *The Vintage Mencken*. New York: Vintage Books, 1956.

Crawford, Tad. *Business and Legal Forms for Authors and Self-Publishers*. New York: Allworth Press, 2000.

Fowler, H. W. *A Dictionary of Modern English Usage*. New York: Oxford University Press, 1983.

Gilman, Mary Louise. *One Word, Two Words, Hyphenated?* National Court Reporter Association, 1998.

Goldberg, Natalie. *Writing Down the Bones: Freeing the Writer Within*. Boston: Shambala Publications, 1986.

Healy, Jane M. *Endangered Minds: Why Our Children Don't Think*. New York: Simon & Schuster, 1990.

Jenkinson, Edward B. *Censors in the Classroom: The Mind Benders*. Carbondale and Edwardsville, Ill.: Southern Illinois University Press, 1979.

Lamott, Anne. *Bird by Bird: Some Instructions on Writing and Life*. New York: Pantheon Books, 1994; Doubleday Anchor Books, 1995.

McCrum, Robert, William Cran, and Robert MacNeil. *The Story of English*. New York: Viking Penguin, 1986.

Marcus, Leonard S., ed. *Dear Genius: The Letters of Ursula Nordstrom*. New York: HarperCollins, 1998.

Merriam-Webster's Collegiate Dictionary. Springfield, Mass.: Merriam-Webster, 1998.

Opie, Robert, Iona Opie, and Brian Alderson. *The Treasures of Childhood: Books, Toys, and Games from the Opie Collection*. New York: Arcade, 1989.

Orwell, George. *A Collection of Essays*. Garden City, N.Y.: Doubleday, 1954.

Phillips, Kathleen C. *How to Write A Story*. New York: Franklin Watts, 1995.

Polking, Kirk, et al., eds. *Writer's Encyclopedia*. Cincinnati: Writer's Digest Books, 1996.

Postman, Neil. *The Disappearance of Childhood*. New York: Dell, 1982.

Raab, Susan Salzman. *An Author's Guide to Children's Book Promotion*. Chappaqua, N.Y.: Raab Associates, 1999.

Seuling, Barbara. *How to Write a Children's Book and Get It Published*. New York: Scribner's, 1991.

Shulevitz, Uri. *Writing with Pictures: How to Write and Illustrate Children's Books*. New York: Watson-Guptill, 1985.

Silvey, Anita, ed. *Children's Books and Their Creators*. Boston: Houghton Mifflin, 1995.

Strunk, William, Jr. *The Elements of Style*. New York: Macmillan, 1959.

Townsend, John Rowe. *Written for Children: An Outline of English-language Children's Literature*. New York: Lippincott, 1983.

Webster's Dictionary of English Usage. Springfield, Mass.: Merriam-Webster, 1993.

Webster's New Dictionary of Synonyms: A Dictionary of Discriminated Synonyms with Antonyms and Analogous and Contrasted Words. Springfield, Mass.: Merriam-Webster, 1994.

INDEX

Index

Index

Index

Index

Index

Index

Index